Role of Management Information System For University Administration

Role Of Management Information System For University Administration

By

R.V. Kulkarni

M. J. Joshi

Ess Ess Publications

4837/24, Ansari Road, Darya Ganj,
New Delhi-110002
✆ : 23260807, 41563444
Fax : 011-41563334
E-mail: info@essessreference.com
url:http://www.essessreference.com

Ess Ess Publications
4837/24, Ansari Road,
Darya Ganj,
New Delhi-110 002.

Tel.: 23260807, 41563444
Fax: 41563334
E-mail: info@essessreference.com
www.essessreference.com

Rs.675/-

First Published - 2007

ISBN: 81-7000-502-7 (10 Digit)
978-81-7000502-5 (13 Digit)

Published By Ess Ess Publications and printed at Salasar Imaging Systems

PRINTED IN INDIA

Preface

Management Information System (MIS) deals with the management of information in an organization using tools and techniques over diverse communication channels, including human resources and information technology. Information Technology (IT), on the other hand, pertains to the study of computer hardware, software and telecommunications and is thus a tool of MIS.

Various studies have revealed that the deployment of information systems can significantly improve the performance of an organization in terms of resource productivity, profitability and services to its business partners. This , however , calls for a strategic alignment of the proposed information system with the organization's business processes, goals and strategy. It is often found that the deployment of information system with improper strategic alignment may not guarantee any such improvement.

Recent advances in information and communication technologies have redefined the role of MIS in an organization from being merely a tool of management reporting to that of business transformation. In developing countries, including India, the teaching and use of MIS has by and large focused on an IT perspective rather than an organizational and strategic perspective. This is undergoing a change as more and more experts and organizations are adopting information systems (IS) for business process transformation and strategic advantages.

A decision support system (DSS) is an information system application that assists decision making. DSS tend to be used in planning, analyzing alternatives, and trial and error search for solutions. DSS are generally operated through terminal-based interactive dialogs with users.

DSS incorporates a variety of decision models. DSS represents a significant class of MIS.

The growth of Internet, the globalization and rise of information economics have raised the importance of information technologies and systems in business and management. Ultimately, these changes are leading to fully digital universities where all internal processes and relationships with students and colleges are digitally enabled. In digital university information support for administrative decisions is available anytime and anywhere in the university.

The Universities, as they are, should be perpetual bodies and they should have the freedom to select their teachers to teach those students whom they decide to admit to the different courses of studies and finally grant 'licenses/degrees to the worthy students at the end of the successful completion of the Courses of Studies. The objective of the university shall be to disseminate, create and preserve knowledge and understanding by teaching, research, extension and service and by effective demonstration and influence of its corporate life on society in general. University has to promote acquisition of knowledge in a rapidly developing and changing society and to continually offer opportunities of upgrading knowledge, training and skills in the context of innovations, research and discovery in all fields of human endeavor by developing higher educational network with use of modern communication media and technologies appropriate for a learning society.

In view of the above, this book makes a serious attempt to provide an in-depth coverage of core concepts along with the practical issues related to various aspects of MIS in the context of the developing world while relating it to the global scenario.

–Authors

Preamble

The management of universities emerges as the key challenge in the 21st Century, particularly in developing countries like India. Effectiveness of any organization, including the university, depends upon its ability to accomplish three essential aims, namely, to achieve its goals, maintain it self internally and adapt to new and ever-changing environment. As a result of financial stringency, coupled with demands for improved efficiency, universities have been forced to reduce expenditure, seek new sources of funding and improve utilization of existing resources. This has necessitated changes in the mechanisms, techniques and styles of university management. Effective functioning of universities in the present era is conditioned by an effective and productive use of the existing resources. Computerization of management may substantially improve efficiency and ensure maximum savings. In view of this, universities are required to change their outlook, as their traditional way of functioning can hardly improve the quality of management. Information Technology has the potential of influencing various organizational processes and management tasks, and the universities ought to adopt it if they have to realize their goals effectively.

The Indian University has undergone remarkable change in the last five decades. There is an all-round growth and expansion in terms of student, staff, course, curriculum and activities, the objectives etc. The share of government in financing higher education has increased to eighty percent of the total expenditure on higher education. This growth/ expansion of higher education has indirectly posed several questions and challenges before management and administration and thus the area needs rethinking and renovation. The administrative work as prevalent in the universities of India is predominately manual in nature. These activities are repetitive and laborious in nature. The rising cost of administrative overhead expenditure and to meet the deadlines with improved quality of work has necessitated for immediate computerization of all administrative activities of the university.

The prosperity of a country is determined by the resources it is endowed with, both material resources as well as human resources. The quality of human resources primarily determines development of a country, which ultimately depends on the level of knowledge, skills and attitudes values of the citizens. In the development of knowledge, the role of higher education is crucial. Universities are the pillars of knowledge and higher education is the façade of a nation. This provides sufficient reason to manage and maintain the universities, which are the providers of Higher Education. Presently in India we have 322 universities which can be categorized into state Universities, Central Universities, Deemed Universities, Institution of National Importance, and Professional Universities etc. The universities have specific structure and well defined functions.

Management is a 'Man / People' based assistance that carry out tasks finalized for the organizations in the stipulated time. Tasks include functions of diversified nature and bear the goal to be achieved. Administration on the other hand is the method and the scope that prepare an enterprise for mastering and serving with efficiency the different aspects of success, to encourage its market value and meet environmental factors in which the business is being carried out with confidence and zeal.

Information Technology is an amalgam of some wonderful inventions of 20th century in the field of electronics and communication technology. In very short span of time it acquired a very important place in the present society affecting almost all aspects of human life. The prime concern of this technology is the better information management and its communication around the globe without hindrance of time and space wherever the information, knowledge and wisdom is concerned the university comes as a generator of all these for the betterment of individual and eventually for society. The university is established for individual building, community building saving national future and to play effective role in global affairs. In this age of information, universities or in broader terms our educational system cannot play effective role without adopting these new means of information management and communication i.e. computers and communication technologies. The university management comprises the student's management, academic management and university administration. Each of these units has quite the defined aims and objectives. The university management differs from management of other government departments, industries and multinational corporations not only in the aims and objectives but also in the nature of work and procedure followed. The computerization or application of information technology in universities has provided a chance to redefine and rectify the procedures, policies, decision-making process etc. to keep pace with the time.

The university being an information / knowledge producing institution needs the computerization and networking to compete with academic community of the rest world. The application of the new means of information management and communication in the university is also essential. The universities need the application of the technologies :

* To accelerate the decision making process for better

planning and administration by eliminating the barriers of time and space in communication

* To avoid the duplicity and to improve the standards of the education, research and development by providing the common forum of discussion to the members of the university and academic community of the world.
* To provide the better exposure of information technology to the society
* To decentralize the university system by ensuring the free flow of information to all at any time anywhere.
* To offer the education at doorstep and for reducing the crowd of students from university campus and in turn to balance the growth rate of universities with the growth rate of population
* To make university system objective, accountable and result oriented
* To develop better co-ordination among university members and also to make university system more transparent
* To reduce the cost and volume of documentation
* To ensure the best possible use of all available resources

Apart from above points, application of information technology in university will certainly bring all the benefits of free flow of information and togetherness.

To evaluate the benefits of the computerization it is necessary to compare the present and projected university management system and study practical applicability of the projected system. To select the most suitable software for defined objectives, comparison between projected university management system and application of the software available in the market. Discussion with software developer is also necessary, as it requires the detailed information about the available software's. Each of its function should be tilled with the guidelines of the requirement that are prepared on the basis of analysis. Computerized university management system should be able to provide the data and information regarding complete university - academics, students, finance and accounts, personnel and library etc. from a single node of the system and this system should be networked with other similar organization. We have to treat university as a whole. The selected application software should be user-friendly, menu driven and easy to use. The software must be cost effective in terms of its present version and also regarding the revision policy. Proper training to concern staff has also to be given.

The size and complexity of universities today call for rapid and efficient methods of planning, communication and analysis of their management functions. It is beyond the capacity of Vice Chancellors to watch personally all the activities that are going on in their institutions. Nevertheless they have to be able to gain an overview of the various components such as staff, students, financial resources, facilities and the environment. Moreover they must be able to integrate effectively all these components into an overall efficient operational system.

Problems and Prospects with Specific Reference to Indian Universities

If we look over the benefits and need of computerization and networking of university management, it brings much bright picture, but when we analyze the present conditions of our universities for application of information technology, it does not give any encouraging view. Here we have to think *computer will change us or we will to change ourselves accordingly*. Will computer open the doors of that golden world for us or we will open the doors of our mind and make ourselves able to face that world. Will computer use us or we will use computers as we like. It is high time to analyze and answer these questions before planning for computerization, because mere installation of computers certainly does not mean the computerization, the actual computerization, which begins after system installation, is quite complex and specially for university management, it is more complex than any other organization. Some of the basic hindrances that must be eliminated may be identified as:

1. **Resources :** competent human resource, material recourse
2. **Infrastructure :** Power supply, communication means
3. **Policies :** Opinion and attitude of decision-makers regarding the perceived role likely impact of computers on the educational system and the society at large.

There is a great thrust of infrastructural development to explore the technology in the university and accordingly in the society.

As we all are aware about the importance of human and material resources for the computerization. Without these two we can not even think about computerization and networking. Unfortunately in our universities we lack both these resources. Being knowledge and information producing organizations it is expected from universities to find out the ways and means to utilize the least resources for best possible uses. The growth and exploration rate of information technology is much higher than any other previous technology. A study shows that

Information Technology had reached to 10 crores people in only three years while Radio had taken 30 and Television 15 years. In addition to it, its application in all walks of life have provided big boost to the consumerism and as a basic principle of this particular phenomenon.

Information Technology can bring revolutionary changes in university management. But the administration in most of the universities has remained indifferent towards introduction of new technology for qualitative and quantitative improvement in the management. It is true that the implementation of innovation and change in university management often faces obstacles and problems, including the internal resistance to change, inadequate staffing or financial resources or insufficient time for developing to preparation and planning to make the change effective. It is time to realize that the use of information technology in higher education can take care of all major problems like equality, quantity, quality and economy, being faced by the Indian universities.

Contents

List of Abbreviations

Abbreviation		*Description*
1.	MIS	Management Information System
2.	EDP	Electronic Data Processing
3.	LAN	Local Area Network
4.	DP	Data Processing
5.	DSS	Decision Support System
6.	IRM	Information Resource Management
7.	OCR	Optical Character Reader
8.	GUI	Graphical User Interface
9.	UGC	University Grants Commission
10.	ERD	Entity Relationship Diagram
11.	DFD	Data Flow Diagram
12.	MNC	Multi National Company
13.	LIU	Light Interface Unit
14.	DDP	Distributed Data Processing
15.	UTP	Unshielded Twisted Pair
16.	RFI	Radio Frequency Induction
17.	EMI	Electro Magnetic Induction
18.	FDDI	Fiber Distributed Data Interface
19.	NIC	Network Interface Card
20.	FIRE	Flexible Intelligent Routing Engine

Introduction

1
Introduction

Abstract

"Information System Interrelated Components working together to collect process, store and disseminate information to support decision making, coordination, control, analysis and visualization in an organization". In this chapter definition, characteristics of MIS are discussed. MIS in Public Undertaking and need and role of MIS is also discussed.

Introduction

Information is a resource which, like un-mined mineral wealth, has no value until extracted, processed and utilized.

Information has become a important resource in all walks of life today. Whether it is industries, commerce, defense, economics or politics, information is needed everywhere for planning and control. It is the sixth resource, the other five being men, machines, material, money and methods. In fact, information at present is one of the ingredients of industrial operations.

Information is the substance on which business decisions are based. Information has come to occupy a very important position in the survival of a business. Information flow is as important to the survival of business as the flow of blood is to the life and survival of an individual. It is observed that business decisions are based on 90% on information and 10% inspiration.

Thus, top management needs right information in the right form, at the right place and at the right time. MIS is powerful tool available to every management to deal with data explosion and information needs.

As quantity and speed with which information is made available to managers increases, the flow of information must become increasingly selective. Modern sophisticated information systems supply both environmental and internally generated information to managers.

An attempt has been made by the researcher to develop a functional model of Management Information System (MIS) for University Administration and cost benefit analysis has been carried out for certain sections of university after implementation of the MIS model. Three universities have been selected from Maharashtra for the purpose of this study.

1.1. Management Information System (MIS)

Information is major societal activity. A significant part of individual's working and personal time is spent recording, searching for, and absorbing information. As much as 80 percent of a typical executive's time is spent in the processing and communication of information. More than 50 percent of the United States work force is employed in jobs that primarily involve some form of information processing. A large proportions of these employees are "knowledge workers"; their duties involve the production and use of information outputs – documents, reports, analyses, plans, etc.

Computers have become an essential part of organizational information processing because of the power of the technology and volume of data to be processed. The application of computers to information processing began in 1954 when one of the first computers was programmed to process payroll. Today, computerized processing of transaction data is a routine activity of large organizations. Moreover, the capability to automate information processing has permitted an expansion in the scope of formalized organizational information use. The current challenge in information processing is to use the capabilities of computers to support knowledge work, including managerial activities and decision-making. The wide variety of computer resources to perform transaction processing, to provide processing for a formal information and reporting system, and to accomplish managerial-decision support are broadly classified as the organization's *management information system* or **MIS**.

MIS is a broad concept rather than a single system. **MIS** applications are designed for a particular knowledge work activity or decision making function. The office use of computer and communication technology to support person-to-person communications and clerical support functions is also included in this chapter as part of management information system.

The design and implementation of management information systems in an organization necessitates the identification of information requirements. The requirements for routine transaction processing tend to be stable and relatively easy to identify; information requirements of management and decision-making activities are more changeable and more difficult to define.

Definition of a Management Information System

There is no consensus on the definition of the term

"management information system". Some writers prefer alternative terminology such as "information processing system," "Information and decision system," "organizational information system," or simply "information system" to refer to the computer-based information processing system which supports the operations, management, and decision-making functions of an organization.

A definition of a management information system, as the term is generally understood, is a *user-machine system for providing information to support operations, management and decision-making functions in an organization.* The *system utilizes computer hardware and software; manual procedures; models for analysis, planning, control and decision-making; and a database.* The fact that it is an integrated system does not mean that it is a single, monolithic structure; rather, it means that the parts fit into an overall design. The elements of the definition are highlighted below.

1.1.1. Definition of A Management Information System

A management information system is

* An integrated user-machine system
* For providing information
* To support the operations, management, analysis and decision-making functions
* In an organization

The system utilizes

* Computer hardware and software
* Manual procedures
* Models for analysis, planning, control, and decision making, and
* A database

The management information system has been described as a pyramid structure (Fig. 1.1) in which the bottom layer consists of information for transaction processing, status inquiries, etc.; the next level consists of information resources in support of day-to-day operations and control; the third level consists of information system resources to aid in tactical planning and decision making for management control; and the top level consists of information resources to support strategic planning and policy making by data provided for lower levels; but new data may also be introduced. For example, some of the information to support management and decision making is provided by the data obtained for transaction processing, while some may be new data about activities external to the organization.

Fig. 1.1 : Management Information System.

In order to further clarify the definition, the following sections elaborated on certain key concepts: the user-machine system, the concept of an integrated system, the need for a database, and the role of planning and decision models. In addition, there is a relationship of MIS with other information system like : Information Resource Management (IRM), Decision Support Systems (DSS), and Data Processing (DP).

1.1.2. Characteristics of MIS

1. Management Orientation is the most significant characteristic of MIS. The system is designed from the top down. This does not mean that the system will be geared to providing information directly to top management; rather it means that the system development starts from an appraisal of management needs and overall business objectives. It is possible that middle management or operating management is the focus of the system, such that there needs are the corner stone on which the system is built.

2. Because of the management-orientation of MIS, it is imperative that management should actively direct, review and participate in the system development efforts, to ensure that the implemented system meets the specifications of the system that was designed. Only one time involvement is not enough. A company without a formal application approval cycle and a management steering committee to determine priorities will never develop a MIS.

3. Although an integrated system and management information system are not synonymous, the integrated concept is a necessary characteristic of a MIS. Integration is significant because of the ability to produce more meaningful information. Integration, in the sense intended here, means taking a comprehensive view or a complete picture took at the interlocking subsystems that operate within a company.

4. Because of the integrated concept of MIS, it is prudent to capture relevant data close to the source where the event occur and use it throughout the functional areas. The common data flow concept supports several of the basic tenets of the system analysis – avoiding duplication, combining similar functions, and simplifying operations wherever possible.

5. Sound system planning is an essential ingredient to successful MIS. MIS does not occur overnight; it takes from three to five years or longer to get established firmly within a company. Therefore, a heavy planning element must be present in MIS development. Plans must include some new development while going towards the integrated new MIS. The practical philosophy is that MIS provides a meaningful direction towards which one strives.

6. Even though the system is viewed as a single entity, it must be broken down into desirable sub-systems that can be implemented one at a time, the breakdown of MIS into meaningful subsystems set the stage for a prioritized implementation. This subsystem analysis is essential for applying boundaries to the problem, thus enabling the designer to focus on manageable entities that can be assigned and computerized by selected systems and programming teams.

7. MIS should be designed or developed with the flexibility to incorporate as many future nuances as possible. It is a fact that despite a careful analysis of future management information needs, it is impossible to determine what is desired three to five years hence. Yet a MIS should be built on a solid databased foundation. It is a good starting point for flexibility.

A feature that often goes with flexibility is case of

use. This means the incorporation of features that make the system readily accessible to a wide range of users and easy to use once they are ready to try it. The MIS should be able to incorporate the best of the improving user windows into the MIS database.

8. The database is the mortar of MIS that holds the functional systems together. Each system requires access to a master file of data covering inventory, personnel, vendors, customers, general ledger, work-in-progress, and so on.

The underlying concept of a database is that data needs to be managed in order to be available for processing and have appropriate quality. This data management includes both software and organization. The software to create and manage a database is a 'data-base management system'. Kanter feels that 'although it is remotely possible to achieve the basic objectives of MIS without a database, thus paying the price of duplicate storage and duplicate file updating, more often than not the data base is the sine qua non of MIS.

9. Another essential feature of MIS is Distributed Data Processing. Simply DDP means that two or more information sub-systems in different locations act in a co-operative fashion. It can be thought of as the delivery system, placing information in the hands of those who need it when they need it. Teleprocessing, networking, or just plain communication systems are an important part of DDP.

10. Particularly in the management control and strategic planning areas, and must be properly managed. It was common in the past to view data processing as an entity in itself performing its own function. MIS, is more than a support for the business; in many instances it is inextricably bound up in the business itself. One of the manifestations of Information Resource Management

(IRM) is that MIS will have a higher reporting relationship in the organization and will become more a part of its executive committee.

11. MIS include all systems that provide information , whether it may be formal or informal system. A formal system is one defined by a procedure. Examples are computer programs and scheduling meetings. An informal system is enacted in response to an unanticipated or non-repetitive even.

12. Modern MIS has the ability to report information about the present and to project into the future – an ability that was generally unavailable before the computer era.

13. MIS managers should recognize the importance of both computer and non-computer information.

14. MIS provides internal as well as environmental information. In comparison to the past, that provided mainly internal informal, the MIS places great value on environmental information. This environmental information is especially important to top-level managers.

15. It is necessary to include operational level employees, such as reservation clerks, typesetters, and tellers who all rely on computer in their work, along with their managers as users of the MIS.

16. The MIS is designed to help the manager make decisions. The intention is not to make decisions for managers, but to provide and information support.

1.1.3. Structure of MIS

Like most complex systems, a MIS can be described in a number of ways, because organisation's MIS is not a distinct activity, separate from its other information systems. Rather it represents a broad framework within which individual information systems or sub-systems fit. Here an information system structure is described in terms of four separate but related classifications:

1. Operating elements.
2. Decision support.
3. Management activity.
4. Organizational function.

1. Operating Elements of An Information System

Operating elements include physical components and its processing functions for an organisational information systems which are hardware, software, database, procedure and operations personnel's. Hardware refers to physical computer equipment and associated devices. Hardware must provide for five major functions – input, output, secondary storage for data and programmes, control processor and communications.

Software is a broad term given to the instructions that direct the operation of the hardware. The software can be classified into two major types: System Software and Application Software.

The database contains all data utilised by application software. The physical existence of stored data is evidenced by the physical storage media (computer tapes, disk packs, diskettes, etc.) used for secondary storage.

Formal operating procedures are physical components because they exist in a physical form such as a manual or instruction booklet. Generally three major types of procedures are required for an information system: (i) User instructions (for users of the application to record data, employ a terminal to enter or retrieve data or use the result), (ii) Instruction for preparation of input by data preparation personnel, (iii) Operating instructions for computer operations personnel.

Operations personnel include computer operations, system analysts, programmers, data preparation personnel, information system management, data administrators, etc.

An information system, through physical components, performs the following processing functions: process transactions, maintain master files, produce reports, process inquiries, process interactive support applications. The user of a MIS provides inputs and receive outputs.

2. MIS Support for Decision-Making :

Decisions vary with respect to the structure that can be provided for making them. A highly structured decision can be pre-planned or pre-specified, whereas a highly unstructured decision cannot. A structured decision can be said to be programmable, in the sense that unambiguous decision rules can be specified in advance. An unstructured decision is said to be non-programmable. The structured, programmable decisions tend to be routine and frequently repeated while the unstructured decision tend to occur with less frequency and tend to be non-routine. Information system support will differ for the both types of decisions. For example, when a decision can be programmed, an organisation can prepare a decision rule or decision procedure. This can be expressed as a set of steps to follow, a flowchart, a decisions table, or a formula. The decision procedure will also specify the information to be acquired before the decision rules are applied. 'Although many highly structured decisions may be completely automated, human review is generally considered desirable.' Example of highly structured decisions are inventory record formulas and rules for granting credit.

The information system requirements for structured decisions are clear and unambiguous procedures for entering the required input data, validation procedures to ensure correct and complete input, processing of the input using the decision logic and output of the programmed decision in a form that is useful for action.

The unstructured decision has no pre-established decision procedure. The support requirements for unstructured decision-making is access to data and a variety of analysis and decision procedures that can be applied to the solution of the problem. The data requirements are not completely known in advance, so data retrieval must allow for adhoc retrieval requests. Interactive decision support systems with generalised inquiry and analysis capabilities are appropriate information system support for unstructured decision-making.

3. MIS Structure based on Management Activity

MIS support management activity- Keeping this in view, the structure of an information system can be classified in terms of a hierarchy of management planning and control activities.

An Overview of Management Information Systems

Table 1.1 : Planning and Control

Level	*Comments*
Strategic Planning	Definition of goals, policies, and general guidelines charting course for organisation. Determination of organisational objectives.
Management Control And Tactical Planning	Acquisition tactics, plant location, new products. Establishment and monitoring of budgets.
Operational Planning and Control	Effective and efficient use of existing facilities and resource to carry out activities within budget constraints.

The table shows that strategic planning deals with long-range considerations while management control and tactical planning has a medium term planning horizon.

The following three sections summarize the characteristics of information system support for the three levels of the hierarchy of management planning and control.

(a) Information systems for operational control

Operational control is the process of ensuring that operational activities are carried out effectively and efficiently. It makes use of pre-established procedures and decision rules. A large percentage of the decisions are programmable. The procedures to follow are generally quite stable. The operating decisions and resulting action usually over short time periods (a day to a week). Individual transactions are often important, so that the operational system must be able to respond to both individual transactions and summaries of transactions.

Processing support for operational control consists of (a) transaction processing, (b) report processing, and (c) inquiry processing. These three types of processing contain various decision-making routines which implement prespecified decision rules or provide output describing the decision which will be taken unless the user responsible oversides it. The data base for operational control and operational decision-making contains primarily internal data generated from transactions.

(b) Information systems for management control

Management control information is required by managers of departments, profit centers, etc. to measure performance, decide on control actions, formulate new decision rules to be applied by operational personnel and allocate resources. Here summary information is needed: it must be processed so that trends may be observed, reasons for performance variances may be understood, and solution may be suggested. The data base for management control consists of two major elements: (a) The data base provided by a operations (b) the plans standards, budgets etc. which define management expectations about performance.

The processing requirements to support management control activities are the following:

I. Planning and budget models to assist managers in finding problems in direction and Preparing and revising plans and budgets. This invalids projections of effects of Current actions .

II. Variance reporting programmes to process scheduled reports showing performance and variance from planned performance or other standards such as competitor's performance.

III. Problem analysis models to analyze data to provide input for decision-making .

IV. Decision models to analyse a problem situation and provide solutions for management evaluation.

V. Inquiry models to assist in responding to inquiries.

The outputs from the management control information system are plans and budgets, scheduled reports, special reports, analyses of problem solutions, decision for review and inquiry responses.

(c) Information systems for strategic planning

The purpose of strategic planning is to develop strategies by which an organisation will be able to achieve its objectives. Such activities do not have to occur on a periodic, regular cycle as do management control activities. Data requirements for strategic planning are generally for processed, summarized data from a variety of sources (internal as well as external data). This database contains some 'hard' facts, but much is based on judgement. Much of the data cannot be collected on a regular basis, and much of it cannot be specified completely in advance. For this reason, it is impossible to have a MIS for strategic planning activities. However, the system is one source of information that can provide substantial aid to the processing of strategic planning. For example, the evaluation of current capabilities is based on internal data generated by operational processing requirements, but it may need to be summarised in a special way for planning use. In the same way, data banks of public information regarding the industry and competitors may be purchased in machine-read form for use with planning and decision models.

(d) MIS Based on Organisation Function

The structure of an information system can also be classified in terms of the organisational functions which use information. Although there is no standard classification of functions, a typical set of functions in a corporation includes production, sales and marketing, finance and accounting, logistics, personnel and information system. Top management can also be considered as a separate system. Each of these functions has unique information needs and each requires information system support designed for it. As discussed earlier, a MIS essentially a federation of information systems that are designed to support the functional sub-systems of the organisation. Each functional sub-system requires applications to perform all information processing related to the functions, although this may involve calling upon a data base, a model base, and some computer programmes which are common to all functional sub-systems. Within each functional sub-system, there will be applications for transaction processing, operational control, managerial control and strategic planning.

After describing MIS structure in terms of support for decision-making, management activity and organizational functions, these approaches have been synthesized into a MIS structure. This is essentially a conceptual framework which describes an existing or planned information system. There is also a physical structure which defines the way an MIS is implemented.

The conceptual structure of an information system consists of a federation of functional sub-systems, each of which is divided into four major information processing components; transaction processing, operational control information system support, management control information system support, and strategic planning information system support. Each of the functional sub-systems of the information system has some unique data files to be accessed by more than one application and need to be available for general retrieval. These files are organized into a general data base management system.

A further amplification of the structure is the introduction of common software. In addition to application programmes written specially for each sub-system, there are common applications which serve multiple functions. Each subsystem has linkages to common applications. There are also many analytical and decision models that can be used by many applications. These form the model base for the information system.. The sub system has unique program and unique files for its basic activities. It shares the use of common applications software, a model base, a data base, and the data base management system. The database management system controls all files in the common data base, and may also be used for storage and retrieval of the files unique to a function. The combination of all sub-systems forms the MIS for the organisation.

The physical structure of an MIS would be identical to the conceptual structure if all applications consisted of completely separate programmes used by only one function, but this is frequently not the case. Substantial economies can be achieved from integrated processing and use of common modules. Integrated processing is achieved by designing several related applications as a single system in order to simplify the inter-connections and reduce the duplication of input. A good example is an order entry system. The recording of an order initiates a sequence of processing, each step using new data but also much of the data from prior processing.

Modularity is the design of an information system as a number of small sets of processing instructions called modules. Some are used only once in a single application: others are used in a large number of applications. The modules can be written and tested separately, allowing more efficient maintenance by identification of the boundaries of the module being changed. The use of modules is thus an application of system principles. The physical structure of an information system is affected by the use of common modules for many processing operations. For example, a common input data validation routine may be used for all applications. If an application consists of major modules for input, input validation, error control, processing, and output the use of a common module for input validation and error control means that no application is complete without using this module.

1.1.4. Management Science And MIS

The application of management science to MIS represents a tremendous advance over the disorganized collection of information and management by experience based on 'feel'. In recent years it has become common to refer to MIS that contains management science models and solution capabilities as management decision support systems. The management science literature is so replete with variety of definitions for the terms and approaches to its use in MIS that it is nearly impossible to name any agreement on how management science is to be analysed or how this science is to be applied to MIS. Infact, 'operation research,' 'management science,' modeling or just 'scientific method,' decision science, system analysis, all represent pretty much the same process. The process, which we call management science, is a sophisticated aid to practical decision-making, directed towards the solution of broad business problems by means of specialized techniques. Management science requires managers to define their problem and assumption carefully, usually in terms that they may be quantified and measured, so that they may achieve better problems on definitions.

Speaking to the layman, management science is concerned with the application of scientific methodology to managerial decision problems. In order to make more effective decisions, models are developed that attempt to explain and predict the impact that decisions have on organisational performance. These explanations and predictions can then be used to aid and assist the manager in carrying all his tasks. Management science is simply a scientific approach to the solution of operational problems. It is concerned with providing management with decision aids or decision rules derived from –

i) a total system orientation

ii) scientific methods of investigation

iii) models of reality, generally based on quantitative measurement and techniques."

They are of the opinion that "basically, management science techniques, employed in conduction with modern computers, provide "programmed" decision-making for the solution of many sub problems in the system. Optimum solution to such sub-problems may be obtained in minutes. This contrasts to rule of thumb, initiative, and approximate solutions on which decision-makers were forced to rely in the past. Without the computational power of the computer, management science techniques usually could not be applied within the time span of realistic operational requirements. Thus the computer and management science combine to free humans from repetitive decision-making, so that they may concentrate on more complex, novel and ill-constructed problems as well as on "non-programmed" decision-making. Some of the pertinent characteristics of management science are as follows :

(i) It takes the orderliness and totality view of a problem so that a relationship can be established among all the factors related to the problem.

(ii) It is the application of mathematical techniques which require the use of computer and other electronic calculators.

(iii) Various elements of problems can be studied only when these can be converted into quantity. The qualitative aspect cannot be analysed by this method.

(iv) In it, models are prepared, which describe the relationship between various factors on which the solution of the problem depends. A model is mathematical or theoretical description of various variables of a system representing some aspects of a problem.

The construction of models mainly depends upon recognizing a problem and then finding a matching technique for its solution. We have explain a general procedure for constructing a models, which is as follows:

(i) Identify and formulate the manager's decision problem in writing.

(ii) Identify the constants, parameters, and variables involved. Define them verbally and then introduce symbols to represent each one.

(iii) Select the variables that appear to be most influential so that the model may be kept as simple as possible. Distinguish between those that are controllable by the manager and those are not.

(iv) State verbal relationships among the variables, based upon known principles, specially gathered data, intuition and reflection. Make assumptions or predications on the behavior of the non-controllable variables.

(v) Construct the model by combining all relationship into a system of symbolic relationships.

(vi) Derive solution from the model.

(vii) Test the model by making predictions from it and checking against real world data.

(viii) Revise the model as and when necessary.

In short, models are the main characteristic of management science. It now appears that most scientific conversations start with a mention of a model. The field of MIS is not exception to it. Model's are a necessity, for both study and design of MIS. In order to make more effective decisions, models can be used to aid and assist the manager in carrying all his tasks. For example, to assist the marketing personnel in best allocating their advertising budget among the products, produced and sold, a model can be developed that explains and predicts the relationship between product sales and advertising expenditures. The model then can be used to test the effects of alternative advertising plans on total sales, or analysing using the model might produce on optimal or most effective allocation of advertising funds among the products sold. Models provide two very important benefits that are closely related to each other but are also distinct. Secondly, models permit us to analyse and experiment with complex situations to a degree that would be impossible by constructing the actual system and its environment.

1.1.5. MIS In Public Undertaking

Information is vital to effective management of all undertakings. It is the life blood of business and is playing an ever increasing important role in the day-to-day management and it is becoming a highly valuable business resource both for planning and control. Generally, in the past, information was undervalued, underestimated and underused. After the human element, information is a manager's most important resource. A major problem facing today's managers is the volume of information crossing their desks. It is so voluminous as to be almost unmanageable; yet, good planning and control over operations via effective decision must be based on a steady flow of quality, up-to-date information.

The prevailing notion that public undertakings suffer from a surfeit of information is largely true. There is in general, a plethora of reports and returns which reach various divisions of a public undertaking. Some of these reports often contain information which is duplicated in others. Co-ordination in matter of collection of information and elimination of redundancy are not often released in practice. What is more serious, the use of information for actual decision-making is, at times, either tardy or altogether lacking. Keeping these points in view, an attempt has been made here to explain the nature and role of management information system in public undertakings.

Nature and Types of Public Undertakings

A public enterprise is "an institution operating a service of an economic or social character, on behalf of the government, but as an independent legal entity, largely autonomous in its management, though responsible to the public through government and parliament, and subject to some direction by the government, equipped on the other hand, with independent and separate funds of its own, and the legal and commercial attributes of a commercial enterprise". The public undertakings are characterized with the following important features:

(i) The ownership of these undertakings vests with the state.

(ii) They operate not only in areas of business and industrial activity but also social service.

(iii) They have their separate legal entity and autonomous character.

(iv) They are accountable to the public through the Government or the Parliament. Government is empowered for issuing direction.

(v) They have their separate and independent funds of their own which means that in most of the cases, the prior sanctions of the parliament is not necessary for their revenue and expenses as it is in case of other government departments.

(vi) Unlike other government departments, the nature of their operation is commercial and usually they are expected to run on business principles. It does not mean that public undertakings are also 'profit-motivated; just like private undertakings. It also does not mean that they do not earn profit. They, of course, earn profit but are not motivated by the profit only. They have got a number of other objectives and obligations to the society to fulfil.

(vii) They are usually set up on a large size. They involve huge capital investment and are time bound in respect of implementation of their targets.

(viii) The ultimate management and control of the public undertakings lie in the hand of the state. Day-do-day operations of the undertaking may be given to the private body but directors and other key posts are always appointed by the government.

1.1.6. Need and Role of MIS

The need for an effective management information system is of paramount concern to the organisation now and in the future. Because the organization does not operate in a vacuum, it must coordinate its operation with the business world. Prime importance is the information about markets in which it operates, current knowledge of its customers and competitors, availability of capital, capabilities of available personnel, and sources of supply. Increasing prices of purchased materials, rising labor costs, and foreign competition signal the need for an information system that describes the organisation's economic environment and co-ordinates the external environment with the internal factors to provide management information.

The MIS, in addition to recognizing environmental trends external to the organisation, must treat changes that have occurred and will yet occur in the internal business environment. Advancements in the behavioral services, continuing developments in management science, and increasing utilisation of paperless computer output terminals must be reflected in the design of the MIS. Interdepartmental approaches have transcended the traditional, functional lines of business in complex systems. Still other advances in development have been made regarding methods, procedures, computer equipment, and data communication equipment. By no means is this listing of internal factors complete, but it does serve to exemplify what is causing the organisation's MIS to change.

The changes taking place inside and outside the organisation generally do not stand alone; each advancement trends to affect and overlap another. As a result, an effective MIS capabilities of the organisation is needed. More frequent and more accurate information leads to better decisions, thereby enhancing managerial and operational efficiency. Varshney is of the opinion that "there have been phenomenal changes in the business world on universal scales. These changes and developments in management thereby and practices have necessitated because of the growing complexities of the modern business enterprises which are characterized by fast increase in size of the organisation, rapidly changing technology, mounting competition in market, change in the manpower scene coupled with many other changes in social, economic and political environment. These developments have brought tremendous pressure on the competence of management of the organisations. Now the only way to survive with the complex organisations in these complex environments is to adopt various modern management concepts and tools." Among these concepts and tools, the MIS is the main which can meet all the demands made on it by the management. Thus, more frequent and more accurate information can be provided by the MIS and that helps in taking better decisions, and enchanting managerial and operational efficiency.

Today a mass of information is being generated by external as well as internal sources. Since 1960, there has been a continuous information explosion. Hence, an organisation must have up-to-date information system which will gather, classify, analyse and process relevant information on the basis of which management can take prompt and sound decisions on all burning management problems. Infact, management information plays a vital role in the performance of managerial functions of planning, implementation and control. To a large extent, the effectiveness of management system depends on having and using the right and adequate information. Simple MIS can meet all the demands of an organisation. If a firm establishes MIS, then it does not require under-cover intelligence methods like industrial espionage or hiring competitive personnel to learn their secrets.

In short, it can be very easily visualised that the need and role for communication of intelligence or information, both internal as well as external, is not only important but is also an integrated part of the modern managerial process. The contribution of an MIS lies in quenching the thirst of the organisations of both the types.

Information systems in Government undertakings are intended to serve the following major decision-making areas:

(i) Support of operational decisions.

(ii) Support of planning or policy decisions.

(iii) Audit and review of Government decisions by parliament, judicial bodies and outside agencies.

1.1.7. Information System and Decision-Making

Decision-making is the prime requirement for the exercise of managerial functions. The management functions involve the process of evaluation, selecting and initiating courses of action. The manager makes decision in establishing objectives. Equally important the manager makes planning, organising, directing and controlling of decisions. Planning requires the manager to evaluate and select from among alternatives for achieving desired objectives as they are integrated with short-to-long-range plans. Similarly, control is heavily decision-oriented because many decisions have to be made to keep organisation activities in line with the predetermined plans.

Because decision-making is the center of the functions comprising the management process, it follows that MIS should also provide an effective approach to assist the manager and operating personnel in making good decisions. For facilitating decision-making, a manager will require information, external and internal, supplied to him selectively and at his call. Only MIS can provide him proper information. 'this information will enable him to :

a) measure the impact of decision-making before or after they are made.

b) Measure the environment, and

c) React in an appropriate time frame-learning the development of problem areas in time to take meaningful action.

Fundamentally, the decision-making process can be viewed from two major perspectives: (a) the quantitative approach, and (b) the qualitative approach. Within a quantitative framework, the account is on determining specific values for all parameters of the problem and solving for a speck value or a range of values.

A leading authority in the contemporary study of decision-making comprises three principal phases: finding occasions for making a decision; finding possible courses of actions; and choosing among courses of actions. The first phase has been described as 'intelligence activity', the second phase as 'design activity; and the third phase as choice activity. Analysis of the process of decision-making has special relevance for a public undertaking where the 'intelligence' of the top management so often threatens to become a matter of political controversy, where the 'design' of available alternatives is subjected to meticulous scrutiny in expert reviews, and where the 'choice' actually exercised by the custodians of public interest may easily be dubbed as (personality oriented and hence) contrary to social interest. The crux of the matter is that decisions arrived at by public undertakings must not only be correct and just; the same must also appear to be correct and just to the people at large". Simon model is relevant to design of the MIS. He has shown the relevance in phases of decision-making process as follows:

Table 1.2 : Decision-making Process and Relevance to MIS

Phases of Decision Making Process	*Explanation*	*Relevance to MIS*
Intelligence	Searching the environment for conditions calling for decision. Raw data is obtained, process and examined for clues that may identify problems.	The search process involves and examination of data both in predefined and in adhoc ways. The MIS should provide both capabilities. The information system itself should scan all data and trigger, a request for human examination of situations apparently calling for attention. Either the MIS or the organisation should provide communication channels for perceived problems to be moved up the organisation until they can be acted upon.

Design	Inventing, developing, and analysing possible course of action. This involves processes to understand the problem, to generate solutions for feasibility.	The MIS should contain decision, models to process data and generate alternate solutions. The models should assist in analysing the alternatives.
Choice	Selecting a particular course of action for those available. A choice is made and implemented.	An MIS is most effective if the results of design are presented in a decision impelling format. When the choice is made, the role of the MIS changes to the collection of data for later feedback and assessment.

The following tables shows two types of decisions-programmed and non-programmed and two general approaches to decision-making involved in them:

Table 1.3 : Methods of Decision-Making

Type of Decision	*Old Habit, Operating*	*Standard Procedure*	*New Management Information System*
Programmed (Repetitive and routine)	Organization Policy	Structure	(include management Science techniques and the computer)
Non-Progra-mmed (one-shot-ill structured)	Judgement, Inside, Training and Learning	Institution Experience	Systematic approach to problem solving and decision-making

When a decision can be programmed, an organisation can prepare a decision or decision procedure. The information system requirements for programmed decision are clear and unambiguous procedures for entering the required input data, validation procedure to ensure correct and complete input, processing of the input using the decision logic, and output of the programmed decision in a form that is useful for action. Infact, about 90 per cent of management decisions of public undertakings are of repetitive and routine nature. In this situation, MIS (computer-based) may be used widely at all levels of management. In case of non-programmed decision, the data requirements are not completely known in advance, so data retrieval must allow for adhoc retrieval results. Interactive decision-making support with generalized inquiry and analysis capabilities are appropriate information system support for unstructured decision-making.

Computer-Based User-Machine System

Conceptually, a management information system can exist without computer, but it is the power of the computer which makes MIS feasible. The question is not whether computers should be in management information systems, but the extent to which information use should be computerized. The concept of a user machine system implies that some tasks are best performed by humans, while others are best done by machine. User of MIS, is any person responsible for entering data, instructing the system, or utilizing the information output of the system. For many problems, the user and the computer form a combined system with results obtained through a set of interactions between the computer and the user.

User-machine interaction is facilitated by operations in which the user's input-output device (usually a visual display terminal) is connected to the computer. The computer can be a personal computer serving only one user or a large computer that serves a number of users through terminals connected by communication lines. The user input-output device permits direct input of data and immediate output of results. For instance a person using the computer interactively in financial planning poses "what if" question by entering input at the terminal keyboard; the results are displayed on the screen in a few seconds.

The computer-based user-machine characteristics of an MIS affect the knowledge requirements of both system developer and system user. "Computer-bases" means that the designer of a management information system must have a knowledge of computers and of their use in information processing. The "user-machine" concept means the systems designer should also understand the capabilities of humans as system components (as information processors) and the behavior of humans as users of information.

Information system applications should not require users to be computer experts. However, users need to be able to specify their information requirements; some understanding of computers, the nature of information, and its use in various management functions aids users in this task.

Integrated System

On-line Management information systems typically provide the basis for integration of organizational information processing. Individual applications within information systems are developed for and by diverse sets of users. If there are no integrating processes and mechanisms, the individual applications may be inconsistent and incompatible. Data items may be specified differently and may not be compatible across applications that use the same data. There may be redundant development of separate applications when actually a single application could serve more than one need. A user wanting to perform analysis using data from two different applications may find the task very difficult and sometimes impossible.

The first step in integration of diverse information system applications is an overall information system plan. Even though application systems are implemented one at a time, their design can be guided by the overall plan, which determines how they fit in with other functions. In essence, the information system is designed as a planned federation of small systems.

Information system integration is also achieved through standards, guidelines, and procedures set by the MIS function. The enforcement of such standards and procedures permits diverse applications to share data, meet audit and control requirements, and be shared by multiple users. For instance, an application may be developed to run on a particular small computer. Standards for integration may dictate that the equipment selected be compatible with existing computers and that the application be designed for communication with the centralized database.

The trend in information system design is toward separate application processing from the data used to support it. The separate database is the mechanism by which data items are integrated across many applications and made consistently available to a variety of users. The need for a database in MIS is discussed below.

Need for a Database

The term "information" and "data" are frequently used interchangeably; however, information is generally defined as data that is meaningful or useful to the recipient. Data items are therefore the raw material for producing information.

The underlying concept of a database is that data needs to be managed in order to be available for processing and have appropriate quality. This data management includes both software and organization. The software to create and manage a database is a *database management system.*

When all access to and use of the database is controlled through a database management system, all applications utilizing a particular data item can access the same data item which is stored in only one place. A single updating of the data item updates it for all uses. Integration through a database management system requires a central authority for the database. The data can be stored in one central computer or dispersed among several computers; the requirement is that, there will be an organizational function to exercise control.

Utilization of Models

It is usually insufficient for human recipients to receive only raw data or even summarized data. Data usually needs to be processed and presented in such a way that the result is directed toward the decision to be made. To do this, processing of data items is based on a decision model. For example, an investment decision relative to new capital expenditures might be processed in terms of a capital expenditure decision model.

Decision models can be used to support different stages in the decision-making process. "Intelligence" models can be use to search for problems and/or opportunities. Models can be used to identify and analyze possible solutions. Choice models such as optimization models may be used to find the most desirable solution.

In other words, multiple approaches are needed to meet a variety of decision situations. The following are some examples of problems and the type of model that might be included in an MIS to aid in analysis in support of decision making.

In a comprehensive information system, the decision maker has available a set of general models that can be applied to many analysis and decision situations plus a set of very specific models for unique decisions. Similar models are available for planning and control.

Models are generally most effective when the manager can use interactive dialog to build a plan or to iterate through several decision choices under different condition.

MIS and Decision Support Systems

A decision support system (DSS) is an information system application that assists decision making. DSS tend to be used in planning, analyzing alternatives, and trial and error search for solutions. They are generally operated through terminal-based interactive dialogs with users. They incorporate a variety of decision models. DSS represent a significant class of MIS.

MIS and Information Resource Management

Information resource management (IRM) is an approach to management based on the concept that information is an organizational resource. Given that view, the task of the information system executive is to manage the resource. The resource is defined very broadly. The scope of IRM includes data communications, word processing, and personal computers as well as traditional data processing. The IRM concept tends to emphasize the organizational effectiveness of the information system resource rather than the technical sophistication or efficiency of the hardware and software. The MIS concept, as defined in this text, includes the resource view of information.

MIS Outputs for Users

The user of a management information system provides inputs and receives outputs. The user's assessment of the information system is therefore dependent somewhat on the ease of input but is primarily based on the usefulness of the output the user sees. The outputs thus form one description of an information system and can be classified as being of five major types:

1. Transaction documents or screens
2. Preplanned reports
3. Preplanned inquiry responses
4. Ad hoc reports and inquiry responses
5. User-machine dialog results

Examples of transaction documents are items such as sales invoices, payroll checks, customer billings, and purchase orders. Transaction documents refer directly to the operations of the organization, while the other types of outputs support management and control of those operations.

Reports, inquiry responses, and dialog results provide four types of information:

1. Monitoring information : The information confirms that action have been taken and reports status in financial or other terms. The information also provides the recipient with background for understanding other reports and analyses. Monitoring information may provide a basis for problem finding and diagnosis and may lead to action, but no action is specified by the information itself.

2. Problem finding information : The information is presented in format that promotes identification of problems. Examples are comparisons between enterprise data and standards (internal standards, industry averages, or competitor data) and projection of current performance to the end of a reporting period.

3. Action information : The information is presented with action specified or implied.

4. Decision support : The report, inquiry, result

or dialog is oriented to performing analysis and making a decision.

Preplanned reports have a regular content and format and are usually run on a regularly scheduled basis. Examples are sales analysis, inventory status, and budget variance reports. Prepared at a given time, they reflect one of three conditions with respect to the time period they cover.

1. They describe status or condition at a point in time (such as inventory status as of January 31, 1985);
2. The summarize what has occurred during a period such as a week, month, or year (e.g. sales during month of March 1985);
3. They present results to date and project to the end of the period (such as a year).

Preplanned inquiries are generally associated with limited output, usually with respect to a small number of items. Inquiries are typically handled online, which means the inquiry is entered and response received immediately via terminal. Since the inquiry has been preplanned, the input format of the inquiry is generally quite simple, and therefore the terminal may be operated directly by the user requesting the information.

1. The user may be provided with a means for preparing and processing the request. The inquiry may, for example, be formulated by use of an inquiry language using either an online terminal or special coding forms for subsequent transcription to machine readable form.
2. An information service (often called an information center) may be available to process ad hoc requests. Specialists staffing the information service aid users to analyze requests and specify the retrieval and

processing necessary to provide the requested data or analysis.

Regardless of how the request is handled, the capability for the system to respond to the inquiry within a reasonable period of time (from a minute to a day) to support the current needs and activities of the organization is crucial.

User-machine dialog differs from reports or inquiries. It is essentially a way information which a user can interact with a model to arrive at an analysis or a solution. User-machine interaction employs a terminal such as a visual display terminal or a stand-alone personal computer plus computer processing of a model such as an analysis, planning or decision model. Examples are site planning models, capital investment analysis models, and portfolio management models.

Backup and Recovery

No matter how large and complex or how simple and small the system, provisions are required to recover from events such as fire, natural disaster, malicious damage, or accident that destroys equipment, software, or data. In addition to these major disasters, there need to be procedures to recover from errors or failures to follow correct procedures. The general approach to recovery is backup by creating copies of the files. Procedures are also established to recreate current processing status using the backup copy and all transactions made subsequent to the last backup. For example, if an error destroys records in a file, backup procedures permit a previous version of a file to be restored and the processing repeated. Examples of backup and recovery provisions are:

* Backup copies of data and software stored off premises

* Arrangements for backup site and facilities and backup supply of forms and other supplies
* Backup and recovery plan

With a microcomputer, backup is less complex but should still be performed. Diskettes or cassettes with data should be copied each night (or other appropriate frequency). The backup copies should be stored in a secure location.

1.2. Review of Literature

Researcher has visited various libraries and Internet sites to study the work done by others in related topic. Researcher has taken a review of following books/journals/ Internet sites :

1. In the book 'University System in India', by D.K. Ghosh published a book in 1983 covering complete information about the history, background, aims, problems, decision making organs and processes and about the constitutional authorities of the system including the permanent functionaries and of course about the teachers and students from whom the system exists.
2. In the book 'University Management and Administration', by Yoginder S. Verma published a book in 1990 covered a through analysis of University system, undertakes humble task of developing a management model for solving management problems and optimally utilising university resources, SOLVE model is a comprehensive university management model, which conceptualises the relationships of different factors in the university system and applies the management science techniques to optimise the results of these relationships.

3. In 1994 Indian Management Academy, Lucknow has published a report on 'Applied Management for Universities and Colleges', in two volumes. Various authors have published their views on management topics. Dr. M.L. Singla has published a note on 'MIS in Publish Sector Undertaking – A perceptual study', and Mr A.R. Hemchandra written on 'Management Information System – Its Impact on organisational performance'.

4. Dr. K.M. Hussain, Professor, New Maxico State University, USA has published a book on 'Studies in Institutional Management in Higher Education', based on presentations made at a professional seminar organised by CERI's programme on Institutional Management in Higher Education in June 1975.

5. In the book 'University Administration in Developing Countries', by A.H. Hommadi in 1984, study of Scientific University Administration techniques and policy, with extremely active involvement of students teachers and administrators of the speedy development of higher education in the Third World.

6. In the book 'Indian University System', Revitalization and Reform', by M.V. Mathur, Ramesh K. Arora, Meena Sogani published in 1994, Issues like Autonomy, Accountability, Governance, Policy making, leadership, bureaucracy, financing, distance education and administration of University Systme.

7. In the book 'Managing Today's University', by Frederick E. Balderston in 1974, share a special concern for the enduring qualities of universities and their contributions to society-citizens and trustees, students and faculty members as well as for

administrators, budget analyst, economists and planners who have specific professional and technical concerns with the subject.

8. An article published in 'University News', by Dr. K.B. Powar on 'Information Technology and Higher Education : The Indian Context', refers the rapid development that have taken place in the field of information technology have paved the way for revolutionary changes in higher education, in terms of both methodologies and concepts. The new technologies have basically provided access to a vast volume of information, helped in handling this information more competently and have consequently assisted in improving both quality and productivity. Evidently if the break-through in information technology are to be fully taken advantage of then there have to be major changes in our policies regarding teaching, research and administration. In short there has to be a revamping of the infrastructure and appropriate changes in procedures and methodologies.

9. In the book 'Computer Technology for Higher Education, A Design Model for a computerizing University, Vol. III, The Canadian Experience' by W. David Chandler, Kaltz, Knuttila, Maguire, stahl; symes Published in 1993. Where this book has attempted to look at how computerization affects universities and the society that they serve from the perspective of two countries situated on opposite sides of the Globe. The goal is to improve the effective utilization of technology within the university system in both Canada and India.

The first, of this three-Volume work, is a design model for use as a planning and implementation tool for the university computerisation process. The model has been jointly developed building upon both the Canadian and Indian experiences of computerisation in higher education. The second and third Volumes present more detail analysis of the research upon which these recommendations are based.

In recent years various research studies have been completed in the area of Management Information System. Most of the studies are concerned with technical aspects of the subjects rather than practical approach for decision making purpose. Different organisations follows different systems for data collection and reporting. Due to the reason one or the other, the study of Design and Development of Management Information System in the decision making process has remained unnoticed. More over most of the studies work at macro level.

Information Sources to the Universities

A number of information sources and networks have been established in India. Some of these, which are relevant to the universities, are briefly described below.

NICNET is a satellite based government informatics network set up by the National Informatics Centre in 1977. Its objective is to connect various ministries/ departments of the central government with those of the states, and also associated semi-government and autonomous organisations and act as a governmental information system. This intracity and intercity computer network presently links twenty cities of the country, with another seventy cities to be added soon. Ultimately the capital of the country will be linked with the state capitals and district headquarters, and even taluka centres.

The Natural Resources Data Management System (NRDMS) of the Department of science and Technology provides computer-oriented resources data management systems at the district level. It has files on different types of natural resources (forest, land, minerals, environment etc), socio-economic characteristics (demography, agriculture, industry, infrastructure etc), and remote sensing data (aerial photographs and satellite imageries).

The National Information System for Science and Technology (NISSAT) is an information system that links sectoral information centers for a variety of products including leather technology, food technology, machine tools, drugs and pharmaceuticals, textiles, chemicals and computer discs and provides factual and numeric information on product, discipline and mission.

An Education and Research Network (ERNET) set up by the Department of Electronics, links computer services at the five Indian Institutes of Technology (Delhi, Kanpur, Kharagpur, Madras and Bombay) , four Indian Institutes of Management (Culcutta, Ahmedabad, Lacknow and Bangalore), the Indian Institute of Science, Bangalore, the National Centre for Software Technology, Bombay, and selected universities.

Other important Indian Information systems include the Defense Science Information Network (DESINET), Agricultural Field Experiment Information System (IASRI), National Management Information System for Science and Technology Sector (NMIS), Water and Power Information System (WAPIS) and Integrated Inventory Information system (IIIS).

During the 1990s a number of library networks have been developed in India linking different libraries in the metropolitan cities. The first to be developed were the Culcutta Library Network (CALIBNET) and the Delhi Library Network (DELNET). These were followed by networks for Bombay (BONET), Madras (MALIBNET), Ahmedabad (ADINET), Pune (PUNENET), Bangalore (BALNET) and Mysore (MYLIBNET). These networks are in the process of creating databases of their holdings and in automating the library activities .

Information and Library Network (INFLIBNET) is an ambitious programme launched by the University Grants Commission in April, 1991. A venture for the pooling, sharing and optimisation of library resources it aims at providing a channel for sharing of resources by the academics in the universities. INFLIBNET will include participants from colleges, universities, R & D institutes, information centers and other centers of higher education. Fifty four universities have been identified for funding for automation during 1993-95, and 15 other have been identified or funding during 1996-97. The INFLIBNET program has provision for funding for computerisation and databases, and for training of staff.

Researcher also visited following Internet Site, of foreign Universities / institutions to study any previous research activities in the same topic, but researcher had not found any related work / information on any of the university site except the various training program / courses on Management Information System.

Some of the information system developed by National Informatics Center (NIC) for Government Undertaking are on next page.

Some of the Internet Sites visited by the Researcher for study purpose –

1. http : //www.sussex.ac.uk University of Sussex
2. http : //www.brunel.ac.uk Brunel University
3. http : //WWW.leeds.ac.uk University of Leeds
4. http ://www.lancs.ac.uk Lancaster University
5. http ://www.abdn.ac.uk University of Aberdeen
6. http ://www.swan.ac.uk University of Wales
7. http ://www.tvu.ac.uk Thames Valley University, London.

Information Systems in Government Undertakings

Information System	User	Details of System
1) A) Customs and Excise Information System	(a) Directorate of Statistics & Intelligence (DSI) (Customs & Central Excise) and customs Houses at major port towns.	The information contained in Bill of Entry (Import Data, has been computerized using latest techniques of data base management system. This facilitates a variety reports on import statistics for the customs houses and India Consolidated Reports for the Central Board Excise and Customs.
B) (Import/Export) Licenses Information System	CCI & E	Contd.....
2) Finance Information System a) Accounts Information System	Controller General of Audit and Accounts	Software packages have been developed of consolidated of major head wise accounts based on pay and accounts system of the Government of India. Also, the detail head-wise expenditure, etc., has been computerized.
b) Budget Information System	CGA and Budget Division of Department of Economic Affairs	Software packages have been developed for grand directory, monitoring of expenditure and

Information System	User	Details of System
		revenue receipts, appropriation of accounts and finance accounts.
c) MIS for Bureau of Public Enterprises	Bureau of Public Enterprises	Computer programmes have been developed of accounts of public sector undertakings.
d) Loan Information System	Various ministries/departments funding the State Governments, public sector undertakings	A software package has been developed which tabulates the defaults in repayment of loans, interests due and defaults thereof, penal interest leviable on such defaults, etc.
e) Information System for Monitoring Finance Position of Companies	Department of Company Affairs	To monitor the financial and legal aspects of the companies, a computer-based MIS is designed. The computer oriented card layout and file design are finalized.
3) Economics Information System	Industries and Mineral Division of Planning Commission; Bureau of Public Enterprises	The industry-wise information system for production, capacity, as well as other information like investors and profitability of respective industries have been developed. Reports providing details

Information System	User	Details of System
		on these aspects are being continuously supplied to IMD, normalized socio-economic index data bank has also been developed to provide relative socio-economic information.
4) Water and Irrigation Information System	a) Central Water Commission (CWC)	All the system development to produce the water year book is tested and put on production. Other programmes for analysis are also put on production.
	b) Ganga Basin Water Resource Organization (GBWRO)	An information system has been developed for GBWRO, software packages have been developed and implemented to produce various reports for GBWRO.
5) Rural Development Information	Department of Rural Development (Ministry of Agriculture)	A software package has been developed and implemented to produce monthly as well as quarterly reports for all the 74 districts under Drought Prone Area Programme.

Information System	User	Details of System
6. Energy Information System	Central Electricity Authority (CEA)	The following software have been developed for the OMI Directorate of CEA.i)Monthly performance report of all power station in the countryii) The daily generation repot of all the power generating units of all the power stations in the country; and iii) Interactive programmes for analysis which utilize the data base created for the above reports.
7) Fertilizer and Chemical Information System	Ministry of Chemicals and Fertilizers	Feasibility study for this system has been completed. A preliminary structure of database has been designed and the implementation work is in progress.
8) Minerals and Metals Information System	a) India Bureau of Mines	The feasibility study for locating a terminal at Indian Bureau of Mines, Nagpur, has been conducted.
	b) Bharat Aluminium Co. Ltd.	A project of statistical analysis of geological data has been carried out.
9) A) Industry (Small Scale and Standards Information	a) Small Scale Industry Development Organization	The computer programmes have been developed for analysis of data

Information System	*User*	*Details of System*
System)		relating to Rural Industries Programme and computation of monthly production index. The development of database for the registration of small-scale industries is in progress. The questionnaire for collecting data from leather industries has been designed.
	b) Indian Standards Institution (ISI)	The database for ISI standards and licenses has been developed and implemented. The computer programme has been developed for generating a keyword index for standards for ISI Handbook 1978.
MRTPC Information System	MRTPC	A feasibility study has been conducted and the projects for computerization are studied.
10) Construction Information System	Ministry of Works and Housing	The development of an urban and regional information system has been taken up.
11) Patents Information System	a) Patent Offices	

Information System	User	Details of System
	b) Industries	A software package for the retrieval of bibliographic information from INPADOC patent data tapes has been developed.
12) Education Information System	a) Ministry of Education, Social Welfare and Culture	A set of computer programmes has been developed to process the data about schools and school attendance. Programmes are also developed to analyse literacy data collected at household literacy survey which is conducted under the National Adult Education Programme.
	b) NCERT	A software package to examine the answers of candidates for National Talent Scholarship has been developed and implemented.
13) Social Sciences Information	Indian Council of Social Science Research	The data base carrying detailed information about social scientists in the country has been developed. The codes for specialization of social scientists have been standardized and created on tape. Also, programmes for

Information System	User	Details of System
		processing data on "Privileges of Scheduled Castes and Scheduled Castes and Scheduled Tribes in Haryana State" –an ICSSR project-have been developed.
14) Health Information System	National Institute of Health and Family Welfare	The feasibility study to look into the computerization needs of the institute has been conducted. The computer programmes have been developed for analysis of data on population.
15) Manpower Information System	a) UPSC	The data base design for storing the information needs of the National Documentation Center has been finalized.The work regarding reorganizing UPSC examination system is almost finalized. The UPSC will utilize the facilities being set by NIC for optical page scanner.
	b) Bureau of Public Enterprises	A Personnel Selection Information System for the upper four slots of executive in public enterprises in the process of development. The coding of

Information System	User	Details of System
		the information is about to be completed and the sample data has been tested on already developed computer programmes.
16) Transport Information System	Central Road Research Institute	A feasibility study is in progress.

8. http ://www.brookes.ac.uk
Oxford Brookes University.

9. http ://www.dundee.ac.uk University of Dundee

10. http ://www.york.ac.uk University of York

11. http ://www.sciencedirect.com
Collection of all Important Journals.

12. http ://www.le.ac.uk University of Leicester

Impact of Computerization of MIS

Any organization undergoes a major cultural change as a result of computerization. The impact of computerization has been measured by studying the individual perceptions regarding management styles, decision making capability etc. following table indicates favorable disposition of the respondents towards various parameters regarding impact of computerisation of MIS in the organisation.

It could be seen from table that computerization had a positive impact on quality, style and capability of decision-making. The work culture also undergoes a positive change with computerisation in the organisation, managers and their decision making process is becoming more and more information based. Availability of timely dependable and accurate information has laid to improvement in decision-making capability of managers:

No.	*Parameter*	*Favorable disposition*
1.	Improvement in decision making capability	66.2%
2.	Influence of Management Style	53.9%
3.	Improvement in quality of decision making	54.5%
4.	Improvement in work culture	85.9%

1.3. Purpose of the Research

1.3.1. Need of MIS in University Administration

Researcher has selected this topic after the detailed study of various books and other material available and the problems of the universities. Researcher has find out following reasons to use MIS in University Administration

1. Less man power with universities due to ban on new appointments of staff by State and Central Government.
2. To get speedy, accurate and reliable information, computerisation of administration is the only tool available with universities.
3. Cost of Hardware is reducing day-by-day.
4. Funding agencies like University Grants Commission are giving more grants for computerisation of universities.
5. To the best of our knowledge and by referring the books, material available and through Internet, not a single university in India or abroad has developed MIS for University Administration.

The prevailing notion that public undertakings suffer from a surfeit of information is largely true. There is, in general, a plethora of reports and returns which reach various divisions of a public undertaking. Some of these reports often contain information which is duplicated in others. Co-ordination in matter of collection of information and elimination of redundancy are not often realized in practice. University being considered as Government undertaking is intended to serve help in the following major decision making areas :

1. Support of operational decisions
2. Support of planning or policy decisions

3. Audit and review of Govt. decisions, judicial bodies and outside agencies

MIS enable the university

* to measure the impact of decision making before or after they are made
* to measure the environment
* to react in an appropriate names in a given time frame learning process to arrive at a meaningful decision.

1.3.2. Problem of Developing MIS in Universities

While developing an MIS for university, following problems may arise in front of university authorities –

1. Cost of MIS software development is very high. E.g. In Pune University, outside party quoted Rs. 1 Lakh per month for software development for MIS.
2. Proper training has to be given to all teaching and non-teaching staff of the university.
3. Lack of funds with universities to purchase hardware.
4. Lack of planning and co-ordination among the various sections of the universities.
5. Employee Unions may oppose the computerisation in university.
6. Procedures to acquire Hardware and Software is very lengthy in Universities.
7. Skilled Technical staff in computers are not available with many universities.
8. In University of Pune, development of MIS failed due to following reasons –
    i. Lack of training to non-teaching staff.
    ii. Software development work is assigned to outside party.

iii. Outside party developing MIS software were deputed less manpower to study and development of MIS.

iv. Lack of planning and co-ordination among the sections.

v. Less funds with Universities.

vi. Resistance from unions for computerisation.

Objectives of Information System

1. To record accurately the requirements for an information system : The users must be able to specify their requirements in a way which both they and the system developers will understand, otherwise the resultant information system will not meet the needs of the users.

2. To provide a systematic method of development in such a way the progress can be effectively monitored : Controlling large-scale project is not easy, and a project which does not meet its deadlines can have serious cost implications for the organization. The provision of checkpoints and well defined stages in a methodology should ensure that project-planning techniques could be effectively applied.

3. To provide an information system within an appropriate time limit and at an acceptable cost : Unless the time spent using some of the techniques included in some methodologies are limited, it is possible to devote an enormous amount of largely unproductive time attempting to achieve perfection. A methodology reflects pragmatic considerations.

4. To produce a system which well documented and easy to maintain : The need for future modifications to the information system is inevitable as a result of changes taking place in the organization. These modifications should be made with the least effect on the rest of the system. This requires good documentation.

5. To provide an indication of any changes which need to be made as early as possible in the development process : As an information system progresses from analysis through design to implementation, the costs associated with making changes increases. Therefore the earlier changes are effected, the better.

6. To provide a system, which is liked by those people, affected by that system : The people affected by the information system, that is, the stakeholders, may include clients, managers, auditors, and users. If a system is liked by the stakeholders, it is more likely that the system will be used and be successful.

2
University System

Abstract

UNIVERSITY SYSTEM means a group of units as part of the organization which works for achieving the objectives of higher education i.e. to train students from the form of 'raw material' into what may be called a 'finished product' of a commonly understood and accepted standard for use of the society at large. In this process, the system serves both the individual as well as the society. In this chapter Researcher has explained inshort the Genepis and Early History of University System in India, Its development in post independence period. Researcher has also explained various bodies, authorities, their duties and University Act 1994, act

2.1. University Development In India

Genesis and Early History

HISTORICALLY, the development of 'University' in India, as understood today, is only 126 years old, the first ones having been established by the British Government in 1857 – one each at Bombay, Calcutta and Madras – along the lines of the then London University. Even for the famous Universities of Oxford and Cambridge in England, from where the idea of University and its customs were brought to India, the examples were the Universities of Paris and Bologna, the 'progenitors' of Universities. Hence, for a proper study of the University development, it becomes necessary that at least a brief historical reference of the origin and development 'University' in Europe be given.

The beginning of 'University' of today can be traced in the twelfth-thirteenth century Europe, when the role of Church, as a religious institution, was important particularly the struggle against the high-handedness of the Church Authorities. Schools at Cathedrals came into being in 1179 following a degree issued by the Third Laterան Council, that all secular Cathedrals should have a master to teach Clerks and poor scholars. Persons, thus trained, were to be granted the approval of the Bishop as Teachers for the purpose of teaching, within the Cathedral precincts. But the Chancellor, as an officer of the Bishop, who was empowered to sanction license "to teach", grew so strong that he could exert the power of 'veto' and sometimes be "venal" and sometimes, would even refuse to issue license to anyone who considered "un-orthodox".

Such high-handedness of the Chancellor gradually germinated discontent among the masters and a stage came when the teachers of masters in such great Cathedral Schools as, Notre Dame in Paris organized themselves with a self-protecting guild or Universities. Came thus into being the 'university of masters. Paris is thus, the example of Oxford and Cambridge. Bologna, a free city in northern Italy, was the other originator of the idea of University which had the 'University of students'. These two originators of University ideas had distinctive features. For example, while Paris had its, 'gild of masters', Bologna had the 'gild of students'. Further, while Paris had the reputation for studies in theology, Bologna was pre-eminent in both Civil and Canon Law. Bologna which had its gild of students, appointed their own Rector, hired and paid their teachers and also decided their courses of studies. In Italy, in course of time, more Universities grew up or four Reggio, Pedua, Siena etc. Over about a period of three or four centuries, the rule for students was replaced by the control of masters.

The Universities thus came into being through the conjunction of so many factors as growth of the Cathedrals, the initiative of the city state, the welcoming charity of monasteries, the brilliance and reputation of teachers like Aberald and John of Salisbury, the interest of the Pope and the King.

Concept of University

The concept of 'University can be put to two tests. The First Test: According to Rashdall, 'University' is a body of 'teachers or scholars', but not a 'place'. The Second Test: Newman has, on the contrary, attached importance to the 'place' which attracted students of every kind. Reshdll's definition seems to be more correct. After all, a student, when he moves out to seek knowledge, should able to drink it from the fountain of knowledge of the teachers. Fundamentally, therefore, to the students, the test of 'University' is the body of 'Teachers or Scholars'.

The Second Test is 'a place', which attracts students of 'every kind'. This by itself, is an implied corroboration of the first test as in order to attract students to transmit knowledge, for which alone the students will flock at a place, the presence of the body of 'Scholars or Teachers' is a pre-requisite. Nevertheless, since the Scholars or Teachers have to have, 'a place' where the students could flock studies of various subjects for fuller development of their faculties, even the second test is maintainable – but only in the context of the first test.

Hence, the word 'University' refers the existence of a corporate body of Teachers or Scholars, a place, where the students would be attracted to drink freely from the fountain of knowledge, provided by the Teachers and, of course, the students for whom the former exists. The Universities, as they are, should be perpetual bodies and they should have the freedom to select their Teachers to teach those students whom they decide to admit to the different courses of studies and finally grant 'licenses' to the worthy students at the end of the successful completion of the Courses of Studies.

Earlier Systems and Institutions – A Comparison

In India, the position was different as advocated by Prof. H.D. Sankalia. Even from the *Upanisadic* times, it had evolved a system of education which could stand comparison, in so far as the essentials are concerned, with similar organizations of the West, known as 'City Schools', 'Stadium General', 'University' etc. In course of time, that system was found prevalent in the *Ashramas, Mathas and Viharas.*

Essentials of a University, as Hastings Rashdall has maintained, were present in India from the time of Buddhist institutions which flourished mainly at Taxila, Nalanda, and Vikramsila. Although Nalanda dates back far before the Christian era, it did not reach the state of glory before the rise of Mahayana Buddhism, at the beginning of the Christian era. Its reputation attracted scholars in the fourth century. Rashdall further maintains that the real ingredients of University, as are acceptable to us, appeared in Europe only from the twelfth and thirteenth centuries. He does not recognise the institutions prior to this period as those having the necessary features of the University. Prof. H. D. Sankalia opined that, in view of the system and organisation needed for a University, in India, it could only be a Buddhist Sangha and to some extent Jaina as the nucleus of a University and not a Hindu or Brahmin Ashrama of a *Rishi*. But Radha Kumud Mookerji holds that the essential ingredients of the Buddhist Education was but a phase of the Ancient Hindu or Brahminical system of education.

The First Universities

With the support of Aukland, Bentinck and Raja Ram Mohan Roy, the principles of education was shaped in the famous Dispatch of the Court of Directors sent to the Governor-General in India on the 19th July, 1854, which inter-alia led to the establishment of the First Universities in India, viz. University of Bombay, University of Calcutta and University of Madras along the lines of the then University of London. Although three separate Acts were passed and brought into force, on 24th January, 1857 for the University of Calcutta, 18th July, 1857 for the University of Bombay and 5th September, 1857 for the University of Madras, they actually started functioning from 1858.

Under the Acts of these first modern Indian Universities, they were to be managed by a Chancellor and a Senate consisting of a Vice-Chancellor and the Fellows to be appointed by the Government. The functions of these Universities were to confer degrees to the candidates who met the requirements, as laid down by these Universities. They were to promote liberal education and senior scholarship and to regulate the studies so as to equip the students in different professions in life.

Of the three Presidency Universities, while the University of Bombay and the University of Madras were to have their Governors as Chancellors, in the case of the Calcutta University, the Governor-General was the

Chancellor. As regards jurisdiction, Bombay served the old Bombay province comprising Sindh, Gujarat, Kathiawar (Saurashtra), Karnatak (without Mysore) as well as Maharashtra excluding Vidarbha; Madras covered the whole of the Southern Region. In the case of the Calcutta University, its jurisdiction extended over the rest of India (as it was then) and from Rangoon to Peshawar.

Initially the type of these Universities was affiliating. To begin with, they had four Departments viz., Arts-cum-Sciences, Law, Medicine and Engineering.

An organised system of higher education was thus introduced in India through the establishment of the three Universities. This at once boosted the pace of development of higher education and consequently more colleges came into being enrolling larger number of students. Following the incentives flowed from the Education Dispatch of 1854, the missionary efforts contributed significantly to the expansion of higher education. Impact of such activities, particularly when combined ones of Roman Catholic and Protestant missionaries were taken into account together they "... exceeded the government output in education remarkably" for they were "...pleased to see legal sanction added to their activities as a result of the recommendations of the Education Dispatch of 1854."

However, on account of the Government's subsequent policy of 'strict neutrality' towards religion, as a result of the proclamation issued by the Queen Victoria, after India was declared part of the British Empire, to the Princes. Chiefs and people of India, the support and assistance that the missionaries were so far receiving following the recommendation of the Education Dispatch of 1854, ceased to flow from the Government resulting in sharp decline in the expansion of education both school and Collegiate

Table 2.1 : Universities established in the pre-independence period.

Sr. No	*University*	*Year of establishment*
1.	University of Calcutta, Calcutta.	1857(January)
2.	University of Bombay, Bombay.	1857(January)
3.	University of Madras, Madras.	1857(September)
4.	Punjab University, Lahore.(now named as Lahore University).	1882
5.	University of Allahabad, Allahabad.	1887
6.	Banaras Hindu University, Varanasi.	1916
7.	Mysore University, Mysore	
8.	Patna University, Patna	1917
9.	Osmania University, Hyderabad.	1918
10.	Aligarh Muslim University, Aligarh.	1920
11.	Lucknow University, Lucknow.	1920
12.	University of Dacca.	1920
13.	University of Delhi, Delhi.	1920
14.	University of Nagpur, Nagpur.	1923
15.	Andhra University, Waltair.	1926
16.	University of Agra, Agra.	1927
17.	Annamalai University, Annamalainagar.	1929
18.	University of Kerala, Kerala	1937
19.	Utkal University, Bhuvaneswar.	1943
20.	University of Saugar, Sagar.	1946
21.	University of Rajasthan, Jaipur.	1947(January)

Universities in post-independence period

In the post-independence period, for a variety of reasons, growth the Universities was rapid, the first being the Punjab University, Chandigarh. The Punjab University was already established in the undivided India, at Lahore, in 1882, which covered the East Punjab as well.

With the division of India and Lahore, being the

head-quarters of the Punjab University falling in the area of the newly created Pakistan, Punjab University had to take re-birth on the divided Indian soil with its headquarter at Chandigarh. It came into being, as a result of promulgation of an Ordinance on the 27th Sept. 1947 setting up the East Punjab University with effect from October1, 1947. The Ordinance was later replaced on November 16, 1947 by the East Punjab University Act of 1947.

Since there was already the Punjab University functioning at Lahore, the name of the new University at Chandigarh had to be made, for the purpose of its proper identity, as the East Punjab University. It is now known as the Punjab University and the original Punjab University at Lahore is now known as the Lahore University.

Growth of Universities was rather fast in the post-independence period for a variety of reasons. In 1949 alone, four Universities came into being – Roorkee, Poona, M.S. University of Baroda and Karnatak. In all 100 new Universities have been established in the post-independence period, bringing the total number of 119.

Specialised Universities

One of the significant characteristics of the new Universities established in the post-independence period is that some are for specialised studies which make a departure from the traditional concept that Universities which meant 'universality of subjects'. The University of Roorkee was established in 1949, from a College of Engineering which has Faculties of Engineering, Science and Architecture. Similarly, more Universities of special characters have also been established e.g. India Kala Sangit Vishwavidyalaya, exclusively devoted to Music and Fine Arts at Khairagarh in Madhya Pradesh, Varaneseya Sanskrit Vishwavidyalaya (now Sampurnanand Sanskrit

Vishwavidyalaya) for Oriental Learning, Agricultural Universities in various States for Agricultural Sciences and Technology, the Kameshwar Singh Darbhanga Sanskrit Vishwavidyalaya in Bihar for the traditional Sanskrit Learning, the Rabindra Bharati University in Calcutta mainly as a University for Dance, Drama and Music and also in Humanities, the Gujarat Ayurveda University, Jamnagar, for the teaching of Ayurveda, the traditional Indian system of medicine.

Specialised Institutions of Higher Learning

Yet another significant new characteristic found in the post-independence period is that, in addition to the Universities of special characters created after 1947, the Government of India has accepted and recognised a number of Institutions of Higher Learning in two distinctive categories. Institutions of the first category are those recognised by the University Grants Commission under Section 3 of its Act, as 'Deemed Universities', the second category of Institutions being those recognised as 'Institutions of National Importance'.

In the first category i.e. 'Deemed Universities', there are at present thirteen Institutions as shown in the Table 2.2.

Most of these Institutions were originally established long before the University Grants Commission came into being in 1956. For example, the Gurukul Kangri Vishwavidyalaya was established in 1900. Indian Agricultural Research Institute in 1905 and the Indian Institute of Science in 1909. The University Grants Commission, however, recognised all these institutions during the period from 1958 to 1981.

There are nine Institutions under the second category i.e. Institutions of National Importance, as shown in the table

Table 2.2 : List of some of the Institutions recognised as 'Deemed Universities'.

Sr.No.	*Name of Institution*
1.	Birla Institute of Technology and Science, Pilani.
2.	Central Institute of English and Foreign Languages, Hyderabad
3.	Gujarat Vidyapith, Ahmedabad.
4.	Gurukul Kanggi Vishwavidyalaya, Haridwar
5.	Gandhigram Rural Institute, Madurai.
6.	Indian Agricultural Research Institute, New Delhi.
7.	Indian institute of Science, Bangalore.
8.	Indian School of Mines, Dhanbad.
9.	Jamia Millia Islamia, New Delhi.
10.	Tata Institute of Social Sciences, Bombay.
11.	School of Planning and Architecture, New Delhi.
12.	Dayalbagh Educational Institute, Agra.
13.	Shri Satya Sai Institute of Higher Learning, Anantapur.
14.	Bharati Vidyapeeth, Pune

Table 2.3 : Institutions of National Importance

Sr. No.	*Name of the Institution*
1.	All-India Institute of Medical Sciences, New Delhi.
2.	Dekshin Bharat Hindi Prachar Sabha, Hyderabad.
3.	Indian Institute of Technology, Mumbai.
4.	Indian Institute of Technology, New Delhi.
5.	Indian Institute of Technology, Kanpur.
6.	Indian Institute of Technology, Madras.
7.	Indian Institute of Technology, Kharagpur.
8.	Indian Statistical Institute, Calcutta.
9.	Post-Graduate Institute Medical Education, Chandigarh.
10.	Indian Institute of Technology, Guwahati.
11.	Sree Chitra Tirunal Institute of Medical Sciences and Technology, Thirunvananthapuram.
12.	Indian Institute of Technology, Roorkee
13.	National Institute of Pharmaceutical Education and Research, Mohali (Punjab).

Except the All-India Institute of Medical Sciences, all the Institutions were in existence from before ranging from two to fifty-two years and were later declared as Institutions of National Importance in the Acts enacted by the Parliament. The All-India Institute of Medical Sciences has been declared as an Institution of National Importance from the year of is inception i.e. 1956.

Table 2.4 : Total Universities in India

	Type of University	*Total*
1.	Central Universities	20
2.	State Universities	211
3.	Open Universities	07
4.	Deemed Universities	105
5.	Institutions Established by State Legislation	05
6.	Total Colleges	10,555

(**Source** : UGC official website www.ugc.ac.in dated 08th January 2007)

As mentioned earlier, there are now 222 Universities in India including sixteen Universities established by the Acts of Parliament and are known as Central Universities.

Open University

In the modern innovative world of learning, the Open University has surely broken new grounds to provide education to those who have interest and ability to continue their education and to study in there 'own time' which has been greatly appreciated and welcomed all over the world. The unique feature of the Open University system is that no formal academic qualification is required for admission to under-graduate course.

The idea of Open University was first mooted and implemented in U.K. in January, 1969. The University is also known as the University of the Air (by which title the project was originally known). The Open University of UK, functions through 13 Regional Offices and about 260 Study Centres located in different parts of the United Kingdom. Each of the Regional Office is responsible for the registered students of its area. Under each of such Regional Office function a number of Study Centres, located generally in the premises of other educational institutions, which provide a central meeting place for the students of that area for Tutorials etc. The Open University, thus, functions through a number of communication channels – (a) correspondence texts, broadcast programmes, notes, articles and assignment sent through post, (b) broadcast by B.B.C through Television and VHF Radio, (c) at Study Centres arranged in rooms in a local school or college where students, tutors and counselors can meet and also where programmes and relays are available.

The proposal of the Government of India to have an Open University along the lines of the Open University of U.K. will be a step to tackle the enormous problems on the higher Education fronts. But to tackle the problem of the magnitude that we have, organisation of a high order with sufficient funds are needed for establishment and maintenance of Regional Offices and Study Centres which in the case of a vast country like ours will be large enough in number, is a sine-qua-non.

Some of the Universities in India have introduced the Open University Programme to extend the benefits to larger number of students. Experiences of these Universities will help take due precautions for establishment of an Open University in India.

State-wise Colleges and Enrolment

Following table presents the position of the State-wise enrolment of higher education with reference to the area of the States, population per-thousand and the number of college in each of such State.

Table 2.5 : State Wise Colleges and Enrolment (Arranged according to Enrolment)

State/ Union Territory		*No. of Colleges*	*Area Sq. Km.*	*Population (in 0000's)*	*Enrolment in higher Education*
1		*2*	*3*	*4*	*5*
1.	Uttar Pradesh	1038	2,94,413	91,248	4,17,568
2.	Maharashtra	1603	3,07,762	52,490	3,44,103
3.	West Bengal	423	87,853	46,371	2,36,449
4.	Madhya Pradesh	793	4,42,841	43,655	1,99,138
5.	Karnataka (Mysore)	1228	191773	30,407	1,74,998
6.	Gujarat	505	1,95,984	27,987	1,74,769
7.	Tamil Nadu	581	39,069	42,661	1,70,530
8.	Andhra Pradesh	1157	2,76,814	45,029	1,43,599
9.	Rajashtan	333	3,42,214	26,903	1,37,432
10.	Bihar	800	1,73,876	58,324	1,25,902
11.	Panjab	250	50,362	13,967	1,12,774
12.	Kerala	284	38,864	222,235	99,975
13.	Delhi	87	1,485	4,424	83,544
14.	Haryana	195	44,222	10,400	60,480
15.	Orissa	604	1,56,782	22,822	46,917
16.	Assam	297	99,714	15,825	41,410
17.	Jammu & Kashmir	57	2,22,236	4,797	18,757
18.	Chandigarh	22	114	266	14,944
19.	Himachal Pradesh	75	55,673	3,497	12,296
20.	Manipur	60	21,356	1,114	7,600
21.	Tripura	21	10,477	1,620	5,488
22.	Meghalaya	29	22,489	1,023	5,488
23.	Goa, Daman & Diu	38	3,813	892	2,324
24.	Pondichery	23	480	490	2,137
25.	Nagaland	28	16,527	530	618
26.	Mizoram	12	-	-	488
27.	Andaman & Nicobar Islands	3	8,293	120	148

28.	Arunachal	7	83,578	463	81
29.	Dadra & Nagar Haveli	-	491	77	-
30.	Lakshadweep	-	32	33	-

Sources : 1. Third All-India Educational Survey of Higher Education pp. 171-200.But figures of enrolment an number of Colleges taken Population for all States is from UGC Annual Report 1997-98

2. For Nos. 1 to 17.for 1973 taken from the Registrar-General of Census. Projected population as per 1971 Census recorded in the above publication.

Maharashtra

This State covers an area of 3,07,762 sq. km. With a population of 5,24,90,000 having 10 Universities, one Institute recognised as Deemed University (Tata Institute of Social Sciences, Bombay) and one Institute of National Importance (Indian Institute of Technology, Bombay). Connected with these 10 universities are 589 colleges/ institutions, covering an enrolment of 3,44,103 students. This figure comes next to the corresponding figure in Uttar Pradesh registering this State as having the second highest higher-education enrolment in the country.

Of the 10 Universities, Nagpur University, which is the second oldest University in the State established next to Bombay, has an enrolment of 46,141 constituting 13.4% of the total higher education enrolment of the State. The number of colleges connected with this University is highest among all the Universities in the State, viz, 140, next to which comes the Poona University having 113 colleges but with more enrolment, 70,130 than Nagpur University.

There was a 2.4% student growth in 1978-79, in the State over 1977-78. Fourteen new colleges were added in the State during 1978-79, which was the largest number of addition of Colleges in the country during 1978-79.

2.2. University Administration Concept

Conceptually, University Administration is different from the general concept of administration as is found in the government departments or in commercial organisations for it has to deal with the emotional, social, physical and intellectual developments of human beings. One hand, the administration has to deal with all the problems arising out of the students' 'needs' and 'behavior' which, by themselves, are multi-dimensional problems of 'resources' and 'ability', on the other hand, it has to communicate, co-operate and collaborate with the teachers of varied emotions who are intellectuals of high degree.

University Administration has, over the years, become extremely complex and there is no controversy that it has many hazards. There is no denial of the fact that the administration is required to face sudden and surcharged situations even for what one may call a trifling matter. Campus politics, intra-personal cliques and conflicts are all contributory factors to the problems of the administration.

Not infrequently, the administration is forced to give instant decisions. Slightest mis-handling of the situation may lead to serious consequences. Decisions in favor of one or one section may have far reaching effects on future actions of the administration.

To meet such situations, the administration needs persons possessing the requisite background, temperament, approach, vision and ability.

Functional Qualities of Administrator

In the University system, much of the administrator's successful performance depends on his relationship with the faculty and students. He should not only have a feel of academics, he should be able to make feel the academics about his sympathetic approach and attitude towards them. Mutuality of respects between administrators and academics is a **sine-qua-non** for healthy atmosphere in the system. Such an atmosphere help both to avoid and tackle problems. As regards students, a general sympathetic attitude should be shown by the Administrations and quick decisions should be given in their problems. Delay in decisions tends to create wrong impressions in their minds.

An administrator who is taken to be partial or prejudicial in his actions, will generally have problems to deal and decide matters. Even his best intentioned decisions may be questioned. Building an image of impartiality is a pre-requisite for smooth functioning as an administrator.

An administrator's job is extremely complex, much more than what it was some years ago. His desirable qualities should be creativity, imagination, courage and, of course, leadership. No administration can escape taking at times unpleasant decisions. It should, however, be the aim of the administrator to accept challenges and convert them into beneficial results of the Institution. In educational administration the work "... does include much that is drudgery and the real challenge is to transmute this drudgery into something of an educational significance."

In administration, irrespective of his expertise, the administrator has "...to take decisions in the areas of ignorance. It is to the mastery of this art-the administration of the unforeseen that his education should be directed". In other words "...it is the art of using other men's minds". But this, by itself, requires skill of a high order without which, the administrator cannot apply his intelligence.

Three Skills of Administrator

Successful administration appears to rests on three basic skills; ...technical, human and conceptual". Though interrelated, yet for analytical purposes, they are being examined separately.

Technical Skill

Technical skill is the most known one required of the people and it "...implies an understanding of, and proficiency in, a specific kind of activity, particularly one involving methods processes, procedures or techniques." It also involves "specialised knowledge, analytical ability within that specialty and facility in the use of the tools and techniques of the specific discipline".

Human Skill

Human skill is the ability of the individual for effective functioning and is primarily concerned with working with people and '...is demonstrated in the way the individual perceives (and recognizes the perception of) his superiors, equals and sub-ordinates, and in the ways he behaves subsequently." Since it is the human being through whom the various skills have to find ways for effective functioning, human skill occupies an important place in this very theory.

Conceptual Skill

Conceptual skill is of vital importance to the Organisation to which the administrator belongs for it means this ability to see the Organisation as a whole and "includes recognizing how the various functions of the organisation depend on one another; and how changes in any one part, affect all the others; and it extends to visualizing the relationship of the individual business to the... the community and the political, social and economic forces of the nation as a whole".

While conceptual skill is a pre-requisite for any administrator in any Organisation, its need will vary in relative importance depending on the responsibility at different levels.

In the University administration too, these three skills together and independently have their utility and impact.

Decision Making

The very system of the University, functions through decisions taken in the various areas of educational administration. At every stage, decisions have to be taken through democratize processes – be it the question of establishment of University Departments of Teaching and Research, appointments of teachers or administrative staff, framing of courses or selection of students.

Decision making in education is a complex problem and despite that "...the decision making process in education, the educational administrator, by and large, depends on his initiative and understanding of situation." Such decision making will always be "...pre-ponderantly subjective" and it is, therefore necessary that the administrator is "...equipped and helped to exercise soundly and effectively".

Formal decisions are taken at the meetings of various authorities and bodies. Even there, where collective wisdom works, the administrator has to 'steer' or provide the 'line of action' to them. In doing so, he must be fully equipped to help the Committee.

Administrative Organisation

Despite its crucial importance and high visibility, administrative wings in the Universities have mostly remained uncured for. It is unfortunate that although the role of administration has continuing impact on the faculty and students, no serious effort has been made to study the problems in proper depth and to offer concrete suggestions to reinforce it, so as to make it more effective as the 'nerve centre' of the University system. Its style of functioning, efficiency and approach, have all direct as well as indirect impact on the 'system' as a whole.

Any failure on the part of the administration for timely recruitment of teachers or to provide facilities to students or to make available the laboratory chemicals or equipment or accommodation have adverse results on the faculty, and ultimately to the students.

Excepting some casual efforts made in this direction by a few Universities, practically no University has looked into the problems of administration as a whole. A number of Universities have departments of Public Administration as well as Management Studies. At least in the case of such Universities, it would have been easier to undertake studies and to suggest measures for rejuvenating and modernizing the administration. But some-how that has not happened.

Role of Organisation

Organisation plays vital role in the theory of management. In the management of higher education, the Registrar's office, or in other words, the Central Office plays very important role which has definite impact on the output of higher education for through the different units of the central office are channelised services to the faculty members and students community. Thus, the strength and weakness of the organisation of the central office have far reaching effects on the total management out-put.

Line Organisation

Of the two basis philosophies of Organisation – Staff and Line – the latter is the commonest form, which is along the Military lines, where the Commander-in-Chief is the top man in the line. It is like a pyramid. In the University system, it is the Vice-Chancellor who is the principal executive head and is responsible for all that happens in the University, as the Commander-in-Chief is for the whole Army. Thus, the organisation set up of the Universities is of 'line' type.

Organisation Structure of University

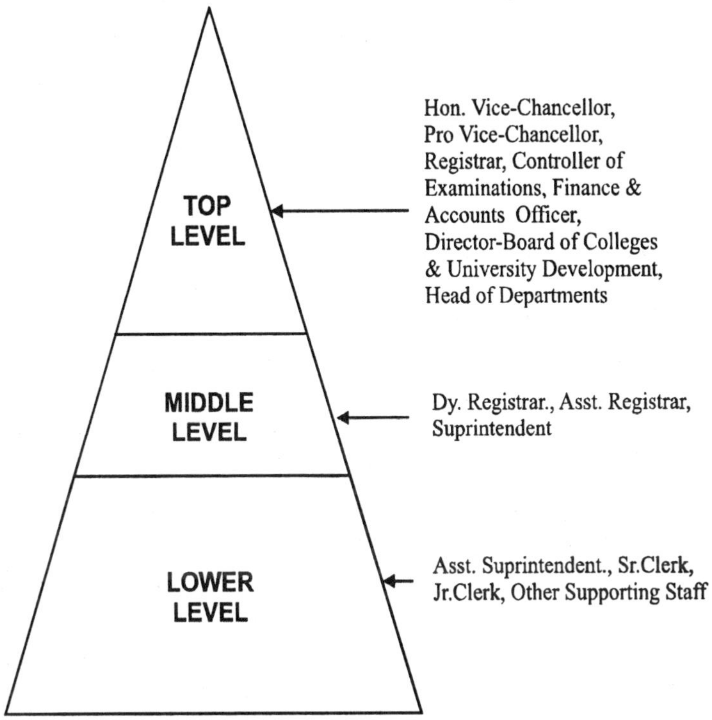

Top Management

1. Hon. Vice-Chancellor
2. Hon. Pro-Vice-Chancellor
3. Controller of Examinations
4. Finance and Accounts Officer

5. Registrar
6. Director, Board of College and University Development
7. Head of Departments.

Middle Management

1. Dy. Registrar
2. Accountant
3. Asst. Registrar
4. Supretendent

Bottom Management

1. Asst. Supretendent
2. Sr. Clerk
3. Jr. Clerk
4. Other Supporting Staff

Staffing Pattern

Organisational set up of the Central Offices of the Universities largely depends on the size of the University concerned for that determines the magnitude of work. For example, a University with smaller number of teaching departments and colleges will naturally have smaller number of teachers on staff, less number of students on roll and still less number of examinees at the university examinations. In such a University, the number of officers and subordinate staff will be less than a University having larger number of teaching departments, colleges, students and examinees for, after all, the office staff has to have a proportion to the total quantum of academic work.

However, there is no strict rule about this. Between universities of somewhat smaller and bigger sizes, the position could even be the other way round also, as there is no defined and prescribed norms for office staff. While size of the staff mainly depends on the magnitude of work of the university, in the matter of the number of staff that a university should employ, much depends on its own plan and financial capacity. If more Sections are created, officers would be more and consequently the subordinate staff. Some of the universities have less number of sections while some have many more for almost the same volume of work.

Neither 'under staffing' nor 'over staffing' is desirable for any organisation. While 'under staffing' has apparent problems 'over staffing' has obvious 'ills' for despite investments, there will be no return. It should be ensured that there is none who is over-loaded on account of 'under staffing' position, allowing thereby to suffer efficiency. 'Over staffing' must also be avoided to make sure that none who is not required is on the pay roll. If there are more people than necessary, the imminent result will be that despite investments, there will not be any return. It has another inherent 'ill'. If there are people who do not have full work-load and are found killing time, but at the same time earning his wages alright, that will have an adverse effect on those who have work and who are sincere. This therefore, has to be taken care of.

All these can be avoided if staffing pattern is prescribed laying down the 'norms' therefor and then to define jobs.

Pre-requisite to prescribing norms is to identify broadly the services to be offered by the administration in the system, for that will determine the volume of work. Once the volume of work of different nature is known, it is easier to prescribe norms for different branches of administration.

Job definition of individual member of the staff should then be laid down specifying the authorities to whom accountable.

Positive Advantage

A positive advantage of clearly written job definition always tells the type of the person needed for the job. For example, neither shy type nor an arrogant type official, even though otherwise efficient, will be suitable for the Information Unit or in the Public Relations Office. But such a person, if otherwise efficient, may prove suitable as a table 'Worker in the Accounts or Examination Section' where there is no dealing with the students or public.

Hierarchy

Every organisation aims at certain goal attainment and for that purpose "...hierarchy is demonstrably the most effective means of maximising the human energy input in task performances". Thus, better the hierarchical position, greater is the possibility of ensuring goal attainment.

The general pattern of the Administrative hierarchy in the University Office is as follows, viz:

1) REGISTRAR
2) FINANCE OFFICER
   CONTROLLER OF EXAMINATIONS
   DEPUTY REGISTRAR
3) ASSISTANT REGISTRAR
4) SECTION OFFICER
   SUPERETENDENT
5) HEAD CLERK
6) OFFICE ASSISTANT
   UPPER DIVISION CLERK
   SENIOR CLERK
7) LOWER DIVISION CLERK
   JUNIOR CLERK

The hierarchy as mentioned above presents a very general picture in the absence of any defined and accepted pattern.

2.3. University Act 1994

Authorities of the University

Object of University.

1. The objects of the university shall be to disseminate, create and preserve knowledge and understanding by teaching, research, extension and service and by effective demonstration and influence of its corporate life on society in general, and in particular the objects shall be-

1. to carry out its responsibility of creation, preservation, and dissemination of knowledge;
2. to promote discipline and the spirit of intellectual inquiry and to dedicate itself as a fearless academic community to the sustained pursuit of excellence;
3. to encourage individuality and diversity within a climate of tolerance and mutual understanding;
4. to promote freedom, secularism, equality and social justice as enshrined in the Constitution of India and to be catalyst in socio-economic transformation by promoting basic attitudes and values of essence to national development;
5. to extend the benefits of knowledge and skills for development of individuals and society by associating the university closely with local and regional problems of development;
6. to carry out social responsibility as an informed and objective critic, to identify and cultivate talent, to train the right kind of leadership in all walks of life and to help younger generation to develop right attitudes, interest and values;

7. to promote equitable distribution of facilities of higher education;
8. to provide for efficient and responsive administration, scientific management and develop organisation of teaching and research;
9. to promote acquisition of knowledge in a rapidly developing and changing society and to continually offer opportunities of upgrading knowledge, training and skills in the context of innovations, research and discovery in all fields of human endeavor by developing higher educational network with use of modern communication media and technologies appropriate for a learning society;
10. to promote national integration and preserve cultural heritage;
11. to develop work culture and promote dignity of labor through applied components in the syllabi;
12. to build up financial self-sufficiency by undertaking academic and allied programmes and resource generative services in a cost-effective manner;
13. to promote better interaction and co-ordination among different universities and colleges by all such means generally to improve the governance of the university and facility it provides for higher education;
14. to generate and promote a sense of self-respect and dignity amongst the weaker sections of the society.
15. to strive to promote competitive merit and excellence as the sole guiding criterion in all academic and other matters relating to students.

Powers and duties of University

2. The University shall have the following powers and duties, namely :-

1. to provide for instruction, teaching and training in such branches of learning and courses of study as the university may, from time to time, determine;
2. to make provision for research and for the advancement and dissemination of knowledge, and generally to cultivate and promote the arts (including the fine arts), commerce, sciences, medicine, engineering, technology, law, physical education, and other branches of learning and culture and their interdisciplinary areas;
3. to make provision to enable conducted and affiliated colleges and recognised institutions to undertake specialized studies;
4. to organise, maintain and manage university departments, laboratories libraries, museums and equipment's for teaching or research;
5. to establish, maintain and manage departments and institutions of research, of specialised studies or of academic services unit;
6. to establish, maintain and manage colleges, institutions, hostels, health centres, auditorial and gymnasiums;
7. to provide for establishment, on the university-campus, of autonomous institutions like inter-university centres, research laboratories, modern instrumentation centres and like centres of learning, set up by the University Grants Commission, Central Government or State Government, which may be used by a university or college or group of universities or colleges:

   Provided that, in the case of any industry or any non Government organisations availing themselves of such facility of a university or such organisations providing the facility to a university, prior approval of the State Government shall be obtained by the university concerned :

8. to provide for establishment of sub-campuses for serving a group of affiliated colleges, and also to provide for and maintain common sources centres in such sub-campuses in the form of libraries, laboratories, computer centres, and the like centres of learning;
9. to create posts of directors, principals, professors, readers, lecturers and other teaching or non-vacation academic posts required by the university with the prior approval of the State Government and to prescribe their qualifications and make appointments thereto;
10. to appoint or recognise persons working in any other university or organisation as adjunct professors, adjunct readers, adjunct lecturers, visiting professors of the university for specified periods;
11. to facilitate mobility of teachers within the university and to other universities with the consent of the teacher concerned;
12. to prescribe the courses of instruction and studies for the various examinations leading to specific degrees and diplomas or certificates;
13. to make provision, wherever feasible, in the university departments, affiliated colleges, institutions, recognised institutions and schools, for survey and collection of statistics, data and other particulars relevant to various developmental activities including State and National plans, evaluation of the developmental schemes with the participation of the students as a part of their curricular activities;
14. to supervise, control and regulate admission of

students for various courses of study in university departments, conducted and affiliated colleges, institutions, schools and recognised institutions;

15. to guide teaching in colleges by deputation of teachers from a pool of teachers of the university and supplement teaching in affiliated colleges for improving their standards;
16. to institute degree and post-graduate diplomas and post-higher secondary diplomas, certificates and other academic distinction on the basis of examinations or by other tests or otherwise;
17. to hold examinations and confer degrees and post-graduate diplomas and award post-higher secondary diplomas and certificates and other academic distinctions on persons who-
    a) unless exempted therefrom in the manner prescribed, have pursued approved courses of study in the university, or in an affiliated college or in an institution or a recognised institution or a school and have passed the examinations prescribed by the university; or
    b) have pursued approved courses of study in the university, or in an affiliated college or in an institution or a recognised institution or a school and have passed the examinations prescribed by the university; or
    c) have engaged in research under conditions provided by Ordinances and Regulations;
18. to confer and award such degrees, diploma and certificate to, and provide for such lectures, instruction and training for, external students, and the students under correspondence and distance education, open university and continuing education courses;

19. to confer honorary degrees or other academic distinctions as prescribed by the Statutes;
20. to lay down the conditions of affiliation of colleges and recognition of institutions taking into account the credibility of the management and the norms of academic performance of colleges, faculties and subjects, as may be laid down, from time to time, and satisfy itself by periodical assessment or otherwise that those condition are fulfilled;
21. to admit to the privileges of the university, affiliated colleges and institutions not maintained by the university and withdraw all or any of those privileges and recognise hostels not maintained by the university and withdraw such recognition, temporarily or permanently;
22. to designate a university department, conducted college, an affiliated college, institution or school as an autonomous university department, conducted college, affiliated college or institution or school, as the case may be, in accordance with the guidelines, if any, laid down by the University Grants Commission;
23. to monitor and evaluate the academic performance of affiliated colleges and recognised institutions for affiliated and periodical accreditation;
24. to inspect, where necessary, affiliated colleges and recognised institutions through suitable machinery established for the purpose, and take measure to ensure that proper standards of instruction, teaching training are maintained by them, and adequate library, laboratory, hospital, workshop and other academic facilities are provided for;
25. to hold and to manage trusts and endowments and institute and award fellowships, travelling

fellowships, scholarships, studentship, meddles and prizes for teachers and students of the university and colleges;

26. to fix, demand and receive or recover such fees and other charges as may be regulated by the Statutes, from time to time;
27. to supervise, control and regulate the conduct and discipline of the student of the university, affiliated colleges, institutions, recognised institutions, schools and hostels;
28. to provide for mobility of students from formal to non-formal stream and vice-versa;
29. to provide facilities for revision or inservice courses for teachers of the university, colleges, schools and institutions;
30. to make arrangements for promoting the healthy atmosphere, corporate life and welfare of the students of the university, colleges, schools and institutions;
31. to make arrangements for prompting welfare of the employees of the university;
32. to co-ordinate and regulate teaching and research in the affiliated colleges and recognised institutions;
33. to provide for the training and quality improvement of teachers and non-teaching employees;
34. to provide for periodical assessment of the performance of teachers and non-teaching employees of the colleges, institutions and university in accordance with the provisions of the Statutes;
35. to regulate and provide for attendance of the teachers on the premises of the university or colleges or institutions during teaching hours and beyond teaching hours, as prescribed and to prohibit

teachers from taking or conducting private tuition or private coaching classes;

36. to provide for conduct and discipline rules of teaching and non-teaching staff and the enforcement thereof;
37. to prescribe Code of conduct for managements;
38. to establish, maintain and manage, whenever necessary-
    a) a printing and publication department;
    b) university extension boards;
    c) information bureaus;
    d) employment guidance bureaus; and
    e) such other activities as may be necessary and possible to fulfil the objects of the university;
39. to make provision for participation of students in –
    (a) the national service scheme;
    (b) the national cadet corps;
    (c) home guards and civil defense;
    (d) the national sports organisation;
    (e) physical and military training;
    (f) extra-mural teaching and research;
    (g) programmes related to adult and continuing education, and extension;
    (h) any other programmes, services or activities directed towards cultural, economic and social betterment as may be necessary and possible to fulfil the objectives of the university;
40. to provide for special training or coaching for competitive examinations, for recruitment to the public services, public undertakings and other competitive employment opportunities, with prior approval of the State Government;

41. to co-operate or collaborate with any other university, institution, authority or organisation for research and advisory services and for such purposes to enter into appropriate arrangement with other universities, institutions, authorities, or organisations to conduct certain courses as the situation may demand;
42. to rescind affiliation granted to colleges;
43. to borrow funds for the purpose of the university on the security of the property of the university, with the prior permission of the State Government;
44. to explore the possibilities of augmenting the resources of the university by exploring or innovating activities such as research and development, constancy, training programmes and providing services for different, clients from industry, trade or any other non-government organisations;
45. to recommend to the State Government to take over, in the public interest, the management of an affiliated college, institution or autonomous college in case where irregularities or commissions or omissions of criminal nature by the management of such college or institution are prima facie evident to the committee of enquiry appointed by the university.
46. to undertake academic collaboration programmes with universities and institutions abroad, with the approval of the State Government;
47. to receive funds for collaboration programmes from foreign agencies subject to rules and regulations of the Central Government and State Government in that behalf.
48. to lay down for teachers and university teachers,

service conditions including code of conduct, workload, norms of performance appraisal, and such other instructions or directions as, in the option of the university, may be necessary in academic matters;

49. to undertake development programmes in higher education, research, consultancy-based projects and training programmes for outside agencies, by charging fees, so as to generate resources;

50. to make special provision for such benefits of the university education to be made available for women students and handicapped students as the university may think necessary;

51. to make special provision for such benefits of the university education to be made available for women students and handicapped students as the university may think necessary;

52. to make special provision for higher education in rural and tribal areas;

53. to implement the national literacy and adult education programme through teachers and students on voluntary basis in the university system and to evolve measures to give due weightage to the efforts and performance of the students in this area in addition to their normal academic performance, and also to evaluate the performance of the teachers in this area;

54. to promote by itself, or in co-operation with other universities the study of Marathi and the use of Marathi as a medium of instruction, study, research and examination;

55. to promote by itself, or in co-operation with other universities or organisations, the study of foreign languages in general and Asian language in particular;

56. to evolve an operational scheme for ensuring accountability of teachers, non-vacation academic and non-teaching staff of the university, institutions and colleges;
57. to provide for joint appointments in single grade of pay in more than one department in the university as also between university research laboratories, university-industry and other bodies;
58. to do all such other acts and things as may be necessary for, or incidental or conducive to, the attainment of all or any of its objects;
59. to comply with and carry out any directives issued by the State Government from time to time, with reference to above powers, duties and responsibilities of the university.

Jurisdiction and admission to privileges of university

3.(1) The territorial limits, within which the powers conferred upon the university by this Act shall be exercised, shall comprise the whole of the university area as specified against the name of such university in the Schedule:

Provided that, the benefit of distance-education courses, correspondence courses, open university courses or external degree courses of any university may, with the prior permission of the State Government, extend and cover the entire area of the State outside the university area.

2. Subject to the provisions of sub-section(3) of the section 3, no educational institution situated within the university area shall, except, with the consent of the university and the sanction of the State Government, be associated in any way with, or seek

admission to any privilege of, any other university established by law:

Provided that, if an educational institution seeks to be associated with, or be admitted to the privileges of, a university, jurisdiction of which is not restricted to any State or area, such association or admission may be permitted by the State Government:

Provided further that if a university, the jurisdiction of which is not restricted to any State or area, wishes to establish a centre or other unit or research in the university area, it may do so with the sanction of the State Government.

3. Any privilege enjoyed by any educational institution within the area of another university before the date on which this Act comes into force, shall not be withdrawn, without the sanction of the State Government.

University open to all irrespective of sex, creed, class, caste, place of birth, religion or opinion

4. (1) No citizen of India shall be excluded from any office of the university or from membership of any of its authorities, bodies or committees, or from appointment to any post, or from admission to any degree, diploma, certificate or other academic distinction or course of study on the ground only of sex, race, creed, class caste, place of birth, religious belief or profession, or political or other opinion:

Provided that, the university may maintain, accredit or recognise any college or institution exclusively for women, or reserved for women.

2. The university shall adopt Government policy and orders, issued, from time to time, in regard to the reservation for Scheduled Castes, Scheduled Tribes and Other Backward Classes for appointment to

different posts of teachers and non-teaching officers and employees and for the purpose of admission of students in the affiliated or conducted colleges, university departments, university institutions or recognised institutions.

3. The university shall adopt the general policy of the State Government in regard to the welfare of various categories of weaker sections of the society and minorities as directed by the State Government from time to time.

Control of State Government and universities

5. (1) Without prior approval of the State Government, the university shall not,-

a) create new posts of teachers, officers or other employees;

b) revise the pay, allowances, post-retirement benefits and other benefits of its teachers, officers and other employees;

c) grant any special pay, allowance or other extra remuneration of any description whatsoever, including ex gratia payment or other benefits having financial implications, to any of its teachers, officers or other employees;

d) divert any earmarked funds received for any purpose other than that for which it is received.

e) transfer by sale or lease immovable property;

f) incur expenditure on any development work from the funds received from the State Government or University Grants Commission or any person or body for the purposes other than the purpose for which the funds are received;

g) take any decision regarding affiliated colleges resulting in increased financial liability, direct or indirect, for the State Government.

2. The University shall be competent to incur expenditure from the funds received from,—

a) various funding agencies without any share of contribution from the State Government;

b) fees for academic programmes started on self-supporting basis;

c) contributions received from the individuals, industries, institutions, organisations or any person whosoever, to further the objectives of the university ;

d) contributions or fees for academic or other services offered by the university;

e) development fund, if any, established by the university; for the purpose of-

i. creation of posts in various categories for specific period;

ii. granting pay, allowances and other benefits to the posts created through its own funds provided those posts are not held by such persons, who are holding the posts for which Government contribution is received;

iii. starting any academic programme on self-supporting basis;

iv. incurring expenditure on any development work, without referring the matter for approval of the State Government provided there is no financial liability direct or indirect, immediate or in future on the State Government.

3) The State Government may in accordance with the provisions contained in this Act, for the purpose of

securing and maintaining uniform standards, by notification in the Official Gazette, prescribe a Standard Code providing for the classification, manner and mode of selection and appointment, absorption of teachers and employees rendered surplus, reservation of posts in favour of members of the Scheduled Castes, Scheduled Tribes and Other Backward Classes, duties, workload, pay, allowances, post-retirement benefits, other benefits, conduct and disciplinary matters and other conditions of service of the officers, teachers and other employees in the affiliated colleges and recognised institutions (other than those managed and maintained by the State Government, Central Government and the local authorities). When such Code is prescribed, the provisions made in the Code shall prevail, and the provisions made in the Statutes, Ordinances, Regulations and Rules made under this Act, for matters included in the Code shall, to the extent to which they are inconsistent with the provisions of the Code, be invalid.

4. In case of failure of the university to exercise powers or perform duties specified in the section 5 or where the university has not exercised such powers or performed such duties adequately; or where there has been a failure to comply with any order issued by the State Government, the State Government may, on making such enquiry as it may deem fit issue a directive to the university for proper exercise of such powers or performance of such duties or comply with the order; and it shall be the duty of the university to comply with such direction.

5. The State Government may carry out test audit or full audit of the accounts of an university, college, school or institution regularly at such intervals as

the State Government may deem fit.

2.4. Officers of the University

(A) The Chancellor

Chancellor and his powers.

6. (1) The Governor of Maharashtra, for the time being, shall be the Chancellor of every university and the Chancellor, by virtue of his office, shall be the Head of the university.

2. The Chancellor, when present shall preside over the Convocation of the university and may issue direction to Vice-Chancellor to convene the meeting of any authority of the university for specific purpose, whenever necessary, and the Vice-Chancellor shall submit the minutes of such meeting to the Chancellor for his perusal.
3. The Chancellor may call for such information and record relating to any affairs of the university and issue such directions thereupon as the management deem fit in the interest of the university and the authorities and officers of the university shall comply with such directions.
4. The Chancellor may, after taking report in writing from the Vice-chancellor, suspend or modify any resolution, order or proceedings of any authority, body committee or officer which, in his opinion, is not in conformity with this Act, Statutes, Ordinance, or Regulations made there under, or is not in the interest of the university and the university authority, body, committee and officer shall comply with the same:

   Provided that, before making any such order, the Chancellor shall call upon the university, authority, body, committee or, as the case may be, officer to show cause why such an order should not be made, and if any cause is shown, within time fixed by the Chancellor, he shall consider the same and wherever he deems it necessary, after consulting the State Government, decide the action to be taken in the matter, and his decision shall be final.

5. Where, in the opinion of the Chancellor, the conduct of any elected or nominated or appointed or co-opted member is detrimental to the smooth functioning of university or any authority or body or committee, he may, after giving such member an opportunity to offer his explanation in writing and after considering such explanation, if any, and satisfying himself that it is necessary so to do, suspend or disqualify such member for such period as he may deem fit.

6. The Chancellor shall exercise such other powers and perform such other duties as may be conferred upon or vested in him by or under this Act.

(B) Other Officers of the University

Other officers of the university .

7. The following shall be the other officers of the university, namely:-

1. the Vice-Chancellor;
2. the Pro-Vice-Chancellor;
3. the Deans of Faculties;
4. the Registrar;
5. the Controller of Examinations;
6. the Director of sub-campuses of the university;
7. the Director, Board of College and University Development;
8. the Librarian of the university library;

9. the Finance and Accounts Officer;
10. the Director of Students' Welfare;
11. such other officers in the service of the university as may be prescribed by Statutes.

Vice-Chancellor and Pro-Vice-Chancellor

8. (1) There shall be a Vice-Chancellor appointed as provided in section 12 who shall be the principal executive and academic officer of the university and ex-officio chairman of the Management Council, Academic Council, Board of Examinations, Finance Committee and Academic Services Committees and shall preside in the absence of the Chancellor at any convocation for conferring degrees and also at any meeting of the senate. His powers and duties shall be as provided in section 14.

2. The Pro-Vice-Chancellor shall be appointed as provided in section 13 and the Pro-Vice-Chancellor, wherever appointed, shall be responsible for duties allotted to him specifically by the Vice-Chancellor with the approval of the Management Council and he shall preside over the meeting of the authorities of the university in the absence of the Vice-Chancellor.
3. Same as otherwise provided the emoluments and, terms and conditions of services of the Vice-Chancellor and Pro-Vice-Chancellor shall be such as may be determined by the State Government, from time to time.
4. The other officers of the university shall be appointed in such manner and exercise such powers and perform such duties as provided in this Chapter.

Appointment of the Vice Chancellor

9.(1) The Vice-Chancellor shall be appointed by the Chancellor in the manner state hereunder:-

(a) There shall be a committee consisting of the following members to recommend suitable names, for appointment of Vice-chancellor, namely

(i) The secretary, incharge of Higer and Technical Education,

(ii) A nominee of the University Grants Commission,

(iii) One member nominated by the Chancellor,

(iv) One member nominated by the Management Council,

(v) One member nominated by the Academic Council :

(b) The Chancellor shall nominate one of them as the Chairman of the Committee;

1. The committee shall recommend a panel of not less than three suitable persons for the consideration of the Chancellor for being appointed as the Vice-Chancellor. The names shall be in alphabetical order without any preference being indicated. The report shall be accompanied by a detailed write-up on suitability for each person included in the panel.

2. The Chancellor may appoint one of the persons included in the panel to be the Vice-Chancellor:

Provided, however, that if the Chancellor does not approve any of the persons so recommended, he may call for a fresh panel either from the same committee or after constitution of a new committee for the purpose, from such new committee.

5. The person appointed as the Vice-Chancellor shall, subject to the terms and conditions of his contract of service, hold office for the contract period of five years from the date on which he enters upon his office or till attaining the age of sixty-five years,

whichever is earlier and shall not be eligible for re-appointment.

The Vice-Chancellor shall be a whole-time salaried officer of the university and receive pay and allowances as determined by the State Government. In addition, he shall be entitled to free furnished residence, a motor car for his use (including its maintenance, repairs and fuel required therefor), with the service of a chauffeur free of charge.

The Vice-Chancellor may be removed from his office if the Chancellor is satisfied that the incumbent,-

(a) has become insane and stands so declared by a competent court;

(b) has been convicted by a court for any offence involving moral turpitude;

(c) has become an undischarged insolvent and stands so declared by a competent court;

(d) has been physically unfit and incapable of discharging functions due to protracted illness or physical disability;

(e) is a member of, or be other associated with, any political party or any organisation which takes part in politics, or is taking part in, or subscribing in aid of, any political movement or activity.

The manner of appointment of Pro-Vice-Chancellor

10. (1) The Chancellor may, in consultation with the Vice-Chancellor, appoint a Pro-Vice Chancellor for the university which has more than 150 affiliated colleges and recognised institutions.

2. The Pro-Vice-Chancellor shall be a person who has held the post of professor, reader or a principal of a college or an institution having not less than 10 years teaching experience;

3. The term Pro-Vice-Chancellor shall be co-terminus

with the term of office of the Vice-Chancellor or till he attains the age of 60 years whichever is earlier.

4. The Pro-Vice-Chancellor shall be a full time salaried officer of the university, and the pay and allowances admissible to him as well as the terms and conditions of his service shall be such as determined by the State Government.

5. When the office of the Pro-Vice-Chancellor falls vacant or when the Pro-Vice-Chancellor is, by reasons of illness or absence or any other cause, unable to perform the duties of his office, the Chancellor, upon the recommendation of the Vice-Chancellor may appoint a suitable person qualified to be appointed as Pro-Vice-Chancellor to officiate as Pro-Vice-Chancellor, till the Pro-Vice-Chancellor resumes office, or a new Pro-Vice-Chancellor, assumes duties, as the case may be;

Powers and Duties of Vice-Chancellor

11. (1) The Vice-Chancellor shall be the principal academic and executive officer of the university responsible for the development of academic programmes of the university. He shall oversee and monitor the administration of the academic programmes and general administration of the university to ensure efficiency and good order of the university.

2. He shall be entitled to be present, with the right to speak , at any meeting of any other authority or body of the university, but shall not be entitled to vote thereat, unless he is Chairman or member of that authority or body.

3. The Vice-Chancellor have the power to convene meetings of any of the authorities, bodies or committees, as and when he considers it necessary so to do.

4. The Vice-Chancellor shall ensure that directions issued by the Chancellor are strictly complied with or, as the case may be, implemented.
5. It shall be the duty of the Vice-Chancellor to ensure that the provisions of the Act, Statutes, Ordinances and Regulations are strictly observed and that the decisions of the authorities, bodies and committees which are not inconsistent with the Act, Statutes, Ordinances or Regulations are properly implemented.
6. The Vice-Chancellor may defer implementation of a decision taken or a resolution passed by any authority, body or committee of the university if, he is of the opinion that the same is not consistent with the provisions of the Act, Statutes, Ordinances or Regulations or that such decision or resolution is not in the interest of the university and at the earliest opportunity refer it back to the, authority body or committee concerned for reconsideration in its next meetings with reasons to be recorded in writing. It differences persist, he shall within a week, giving reasons submit it to the Chancellor for decision and inform about having done so to the members of the authority, body or committee concerned. After receipt of the decision of the Chancellor, the Vice-Chancellor shall take the action as directed by the Chancellor and inform the authority, body or committee concerned accordingly.
7. If there are reasonable grounds for the Vice-Chancellor to believe that there is an emergency which requires immediate action to be taken, he shall take such action, as he thinks necessary, and shall at the earliest opportunity, report in writing the grounds for his belief that there was an emergency, and the action taken by him, to such

authority or body as would, in the ordinary course, have dealt with the matter. In the event of a difference arising between the Vice-Chancellor and the authority or body whether there was in fact an emergency, or on the action taken (where such action does not affect any person in the service of the University), or on both, the matter shall be referred to the Chancellor whose decision shall be final:

Provided that, where any such action taken by the Vice-Chancellor affects any person in the service of the university, such person shall be entitled to prefer, within thirty days from the date on which he receives notice of such action, an appeal to the Management Council.

8. Where any matter is required to be regulated by the Status, Ordinances or Regulations, but no Statutes, Ordinances or Regulations are made in that behalf the Vice-Chancellor may, for the time being, regulate matter by issuing such directions as he thinks necessary, and shall, at the earliest opportunity thereafter, place them before the Management Council or other authority or body concerned for approval. He may, at the same time, place before such authority or body for consideration the draft of the Statutes, Ordinances or Regulations, as the case may be, required to be made in that behalf.

9. The Vice-Chancellor shall be the appointing authority for the university teachers on the recommendations of the selection committee constituted for the said purpose.

10. The Vice-Chancellor shall be the appointing authority for officers of the university of the rank of Assistant Registrar and of the rank equivalent thereto and above.

11. As the Chairman of the Authorities or bodies or committees of the university the Vice-Chancellor shall be empowered to suspend a member from the meeting of the authority, body or committee for persisting to obstruct or stall the proceedings or for indulging in behavior unbecoming of a member, and shall report the matter accordingly, to the Chancellor.

12. The Vice-Chancellor shall place before the Management Council a report of the work of the university periodically as provided under the Ordinances.

13. The Vice-Chancellor shall exercise such other powers and perform such other duties as may be conferred upon him by or under the Act.

14. (a) The Vice-Chancellor shall have the right to cause an inspection to be made by such person or persons or body of persons as he may direct, of the university, its buildings, laboratories, libraries, museums, workshops and equipment's and of any institution, affiliated, conducted or autonomous college, hall or hostel maintained or recognised by the university, and of the examination, teachings and other work conducted by or on behalf of the university, and to cause an inquiry to be made in a like manner regarding any matter connected with the administration or finance of the university, affiliated college or recognised institutions :

    Provided that, the Vice-Chancellor shall, in the case of affiliated college or recognised institution, give notice to the management of such affiliated college or recognised institution of his intention to cause an inspection or an inquiry to be so made :

Provided further that, the management shall have right to make such representation to the Vice-Chancellor as it thinks necessary before such inspection or inquiry is made;

(b) after considering such representation, if any made, the Vice-Chancellor may cause such inspection or inquiry to be made or may drop the same;

(c) in the case of management when an inspection or inquiry has been caused to be made, the management, shall be entitled to appoint a representative, who shall have the right to be present and be heard at such inspection or inquiry;

(d) the Vice-Chancellor may, if the inspection or inquiry is made regarding any college or institution admitted to the privileges of the university, communicate to the management the result of such inspection or inquiry;

(e) the management shall communicate to the Vice-Chancellor such action, if any, as it proposes to take or has been taken by it;

(f) where the management, does not, within the time fixed by the Vice-Chancellor, take action to his satisfaction, the Vice-Chancellor shall place before the Management Council the inspection or inquiry report and explanation furnished or representation made by the management, for its consideration.

12. (1) There shall be a Dean for each faculty. He shall be an academic officer of the university concerned with and responsible for implementation of the academic policies approved by the Academic Council in respect of academic development, maintenance of standards of teaching and research and training of teacher within his faculty.

2. The Dean of every faculty shall be elected by the members of the faculty from amongst themselves.
3. The Dean shall convene meetings of the faculty, as and when required, in consultation with the Vice-Chancellor and shall preside over the same. He shall formulate the policies and development programme of the faculty and present the same to the appropriate authorities for their consideration.
4. The Dean shall be responsible for the academic development of the faculty and shall ensure proper implementation of the decisions of the Management Council, Academic Council, Board of College and University Development and the Board of Examinations in respect of his faculty and the decisions of the faculty and the Boards of Studies under his purview.
5. Subject to the superintendence, direction and control of the Vice-Chancellor, the Dean shall, after taking such advice as he thinks necessary, decide upon the grievances of students regarding the enrolment, eligibility, migration, scholarships, studentships or freeships, grant of terms, admission to university examinations.
6. The Dean shall Enquirer, on being directed by the Academic Council, into any malpractice related to any academic programme in his faculty by a university department, affiliated or conducted college or recognised institution and report the findings to the Academic Council.
7. The Dean shall prepare proposals for the award of fellowships, scholarships and other distinctions in his faculty for submission to the Academic Council.

Director of Board of College and University Development.

13.(1) The Director of the Board of College and University Development shall be nominated by the Vice-Chancellor, from amongst professors of the university, institutions or departments or principals.

2. The Director shall be,

(a) *the principal academic planning and academic audit officer for the academic development programmes, including post-graduate teaching, research and extension programmes and collaborative programmes of the university;*

(b) *the Secretary of the Board of College and University Development and shall conduct academic audit of university departments or institutions, recognised institutions, post-graduate centres and affiliated colleges;*

(c) *responsible for ensuring that the decisions of the Board for long-term and short-term development plans of the university and its affiliated colleges in their academic programmes are duly processed and implemented through relevant authorities, bodies, committees and officers;*

(d) *the principal liaison officer with the external funding agencies for generating funds for the collaborative and development programmes of the university and monitor their proper utilization;*

(e) *responsible for establishing liaison for fostering and promoting collaboration between the university, colleges and national and international institutions and scientific, industrial and commercial organisations;*

(f) *responsible for submitting an annual report on the progress achieved in different developmental and collaborative programmes to the Vice-Chancellor who shall place the same before the Management Council.*

Registrar

14. (1) The Registrar shall be appointed by the Vice-Chancellor on the recommendation of a selection committee constituted for the purpose.

2. The Registrar shall be the Chief Administrative Officer of the university. He shall be a full-time salaried officer and shall work directly under the superintendence, direction and control of the Vice-Chancellor.
3. Appointment of the Registrar shall be for a term of five years and he shall be eligible for reappointment. The qualifications and experience for the purpose of selection of the Registrar shall be as laid down by the University Grants Commission and approved by the State Government.
4. When the office of the Registrar falls vacant or when the Registrar is, by reason of illness or absence or any other cause, unable to perform the duties of his office for a period not exceeding six months, the Vice-Chancellor shall appoint a suitable person to officiate as the Registrar until a new Registrar is appointed and assumes office or the Registrar resumes duty, as the case may be.
5. The Registrar shall act as Secretary of the Senate, Management Council, Academic Council and such other authorities, bodies and committees as prescribed by or under this Act.
6. The Registrar shall be the appointing and the disciplinary authority of the employees of the

university other than the teachers, non-vacation academic staff and officers of the rank of Assistant Registrar and other officers holding posts equivalent thereto or above. An appeal by a person aggrieved by the decision of the Registrar may be preferred within thirty days from the date of communication of such decision, to the Vice-Chancellor.

7. Subject to the decisions of the authorities of the university, the Registrar shall have the power to enter into agreements, sign documents and authenticate records on behalf of the university.
8. The Registrar shall be the custodian of the records the common seal and such other property of the university as the Management Council may, commit to his charge.
9. The Registrar shall conduct elections as per the programme approved by the Vice-Chancellor.
10. The Registrar shall prepare and update the Handbook of the Statutes, Ordinances and Regulations approved by the authorities, bodies or committees from time to time, and make them available to all the respective members of the authorities and officers of the university.
11. The Registrar shall receive complaints and suggestions in regard to the improvement of administration and consider them for appropriate action.
12. The Registrar shall exercise such other powers and perform such other duties as prescribed by or under the Act or assigned to him, from time to time, by the Vice-Chancellor.

Controller of Examinations

15. (1) (a) Controller of Examinations shall be appointed by the Vice-Chancellor on the recommendations of a selection committee constituted for the purpose;

(b) the Controller of Examinations shall be the principal officer-in-charge of the conduct of exam and tests of the university and declaration of their results. He shall discharge his functions under the superintendence, direction and guidance of the Board of Examinations. He shall be a full-time salaried officer of the university and shall work directly under the control of the Vice-Chancellor.

(c) his appointment shall be for a term of five years, and he shall be eligible for re-appointment. The qualifications and experience for the purpose of selection of the Controller shall be such as may be prescribed.

2. The Controller shall be the Member-Secretary of the Board of Examinations and of the committees appointed by the board except the committees constituted under section 32(5)(a) for appointment of paper-setters, examiners and moderators. He shall be responsible for prompt and proper implementation of their decisions.

3. Without prejudice to the generality of the provisions of sub-section (1)(b), the controller shall be responsible for making all arrangements necessary for holding examinations and tests and declaration of results. It shall be his responsibility,-

(a) to prepare and announce in advance the calendar of examinations;

(b) to arrange for printing of question papers;

(c) to arrange to get performance of the candidates at the examinations properly assessed, and process the results;

(d) to arrange for the timely publication of results

of examinations and other tests;

(e) to postpone or cancel examinations, in part or in whole, in the event of malpractice's or if the circumstances so wàrrant, and take disciplinary action or initiate any civil or criminal proceedings against any person or a group of persons or a college or an institution alleged to have committed malpractice's;

(f) to take disciplinary action where necessary against the candidates paper-setters, examiners, moderators, or any persons connected with examinations and found guilty of malpractice's in relation to the examinations;

(g) to review from time to time, the results of university examinations and forward reports thereon to the Academic Council.

4. The controller shall exercise such other powers and perform such other duties as may be presented or assigned to him, from time to time by the Board of Examinations.

The Finance and Accounts Officer

17.(1)(a) The Finance and Accounts Officer shall be the principal finance, accounts and audit officer of the university. He shall be full-time salaried officer and shall work directly under the control of the Vice-Chancellor;

(b) The Finance Officer shall be appointed by the Management Council either by nomination or by obtaining the services of a suitable officer on deputation from the Government of India or the State Government .

2. The Finance and Accounts Officer shall be the Member-Secretary of Finance and Accounts Committee. He shall have the right to be present, speak and otherwise take part in the proceedings of

the Management Council on matters which have financial implications but shall not be entitled to vote.

3. The Finance and Accounts Officer shall maintain minutes of the meetings of Finance and Accounts Committee and the committees appointed by the Finance and Accounts Committee.

4. The Finance and Accounts Officer shall be responsible for presenting the annual budget, statement of accounts and audit reports, to the Finance and Accounts Committee and to the Management Council.

5. The duties of the Finance and Accounts Officer shall be to-

   (a) exercise general supervision over the funds of the university, and shall advise the Vice-Chancellor as regards the finances of the university ;

   (b) hold and manage the funds, property and investments, including trust and endowed property, for furthering any of the objects of the university ;

   (c) ensure that the limits fixed by the university for recurring and non-recurring expenditure for a year are not exceeded, and that all allocations are expended for the purposes for which they are granted or allotted;

   (d) keep watch on the state of the cash and bank balances and of investments;

   (e) keep watch on the progress of collection of revenue and advise the Vice-Chancellor on the methods to be employed for collection;

   (f) have the accounts of the university audited regularly;

(g) ensure that the registers of buildings, land, equipment and machinery are maintained up-to-date and that the stock taking of equipments and other consumable materials in all offices, colleges, workshops and stores of the university is conducted regularly;

(h) proposal to the Vice-Chancellor that explanation be called for unauthorised expenditure or other financial irregularities from any academic member of university ;

(i) propose to the registrar that explanation be called from any non-academic member for unauthorised expenditure or irregularities in any particular case, and recommend disciplinary action against the persons at fault;

(j) call for from any office, centre, laboratory, college, department of the university or university institution, for any information and returns that he thinks necessary for the proper discharge of his financial responsibilities: and

(k) exercise such other powers, perform such other duties, and discharge such other financial functions as are assigned to him by the Vice-Chancellor or are prescribed by the Ordinances.

Officers, members of authorities, bodies and employees of university as public servant

18. All salaried officers, members of the authorities, committees or bodies teachers of the university and other employees of the university, shall be deemed to be public servants within the meaning of section 21 of the Indian Penal Code.

2.5. Authorities of the University

Authorities of the university

19. The following shall be the authorities of the university, namely:-

1. the Senate,
2. the Management Council,
3. the Academic Council,
4. the Faculty,
5. the Board of College and University Development,
6. the Board of Studies,
7. the Board of Inter-disciplinary studies,
8. the Board of Examinations,
9. the Board of Adult and Continuing Education and Extension Services,
10. the Students' Council,
11. such other bodies of the university as are designated by the Satutes to be the authorities of the university.

Senate

20. (1) The Senate shall be the principal authority for all financial estimates and budgetary appropriations and for providing social feedback to the university on current and future academic programmes.

2. The Senate shall consists of the following members, namely :-
    (a) the Chancellor;
    (b) the Vice-Chancellor;
    (c) the Pro-Vice-Chancellor ;
    (d) the Director of Higher Education or his nominee not below
    (e) the rank of Joint Director;
    (f) the Director of Technical Education;

(g) the Director of Medical Education;

(h) the Director, Board of College and University Development;

(i) the Director of Students' Welfare;

(j) the Librarian of the University Library;

(k) one head of the Academic Services Units of the university, by

(l) rotation as prescribed;

(m) the Director of Adult and Continuing Education and

(n) Extension Services ;

(o) fifteen principals of the affiliated, conducted and autonomous

(p) colleges, elected the electoral college consisting of principals;

(q) five representatives of the managements of affiliated colleges

(r) or recognised institutions elected by the electoral college consisting of Chairman or President or the representative of the Managements as the management may recommend. Where a management conducts one or more colleges or institutions, only one Chairman or President or representative of such management as the case may be, shall be the member of the electoral college;

(s) the President and the Secretary of the University's Students'

(t) Council;

(u) the Registrar, who shall act as the Secretary of the Senate;

(v) twenty teachers having teaching experience of

not less than

(w) five years other than heads of university departments or university institutions or principals or heads of recognised institutions, elected by the teachers from amongst themselves, these seats being allotted facultywise proportionately but voting to be in common;

(x) two members of the State Legislative Assembly and two

(y) members of the State Legislative Council, elected by the respective House of the State Legislature, of which they are members;

(z) ten members from the registered graduates of the university

(aa) (no being persons from amongst any of foregoing categories of members) elected by electoral college constituted in accordance with sub-section (5) of section 99 of whom three members shall be one each from the Scheduled Castes, Scheduled Tribes and Other Backward Classes;

(bb) six persons, nominated by the Chancellor, who shall include

(cc) distinguished educationists, scholars, social workers, women, persons belonging to the minorities, backward communities, industry and professions;

(dd) three persons from amongst the heads of recognised

(ee) institutions, nominated by the Chancellor;

(ff) three persons from amongst heads of the university

(gg) departments or of the university institutions not

below the rank of reader, nominated by the Vice-Chancellor ;

(hh) deans of faculties;

(ii) two persons, nominated by the Vice-Chancellor one of whom

(jj) shall be an employee of the university and the other shall be from amongst the employees of the affiliated colleges or recognised institutions other than university teachers, registrars, deputy registrars, assistant registrars;

(kk) one representative of the donor-individuals or donor

(ll) organisations, nominated by the Chancellor.

2. The Chancellor shall normally preside over the Senate and in his absence the Vice-Chancellor shall preside.

3. The Senate shall meet at least twice a year on the date to be fixed by the Chancellor. One of the meetings shall be the annual meeting.

Functions and duties of Senate

24. (1) The Senate transact the following business at its annual meeting, namely:-

(a) *review current academic programmes and collaborative programmes;*

(b) *suggest new academic programmes consistent with the societal requirements in higher education;*

(c) *suggest measures for improvement and development of the university ;*

(d) *suggest institution of new degrees, diplomas, certificates and other academic distinctions; and*

(e) *confer, on recommendations of the Management*

Council, honorary degrees or other academic distinctions.

2. The Senate shall receive, discuss and approve the annual reports, accounts and audit reports of the university.
3. The Senate shall review broad policies and programmes of the university and suggest measures for its improvement and development.

Management Council

25. (1) The Management Council shall be the principal executive authority to formulate statues and forward the same to the Senate for approval and make Ordinances to administer the affairs of the university and shall carry out all such duties which are not specifically assigned to any other authority. It shall consist of the following members, namely :-

(a) the Vice-Chancellor; Chairman;

(b) the Pro-Vice-Chancellor, if any;

(c) one Dean, nominated by the Senate;

(d) one person nominated by the Chancellor;

(e) the Secretary, Higher Education or his nominee not below the rank of Deputy Secretary or Joint Director of Higher Education;

(f) the Director of Technical Education or his nominee not below the rank of Joint Director.

(g) the director of higher education or his nominee not below the rank of joint director of higher education;

(h) one head or director, nominated by the senate, from amongst the heads or directors of university departments or university institutions;

(i) the director, board of college and university development;

(j) one principal, elected by the senate from amongst the principals, who are members of the senate;

(k) one teacher from the university department or university institutions with ten years post-graduate teaching experience, who is not a head or director of university department or university institution, elected by the senate from amongst the teachers, who are members of the senate;

(l) two teachers from amongst the teachers of the affiliated colleges with sixteen years teaching experience, who is not a principal, elected by the Senate from amongst the teachers of the affiliated colleges who are members of the Senate;

(m) one person, who is not a Dean, Head or Director of university department, principal, teacher or student member, elected by the Senate from amongst its members.

(n) three persons elected by the Academic Council from amongst its members as prescribed by Statute:

Provided that not more that one person shall be from one faculty as prescribed by the Statutes.

2. The Registrar of the university shall be ex officio Secretary of the Management Council, but shall not have the right to vote.

3. The Finance and Accounts Officer and the Controller of Examinations shall be permanent invitees of the Council, but they shall have no right to vote.

4. There shall be not less than four meetings of the Management Council in a year and the rules of procedure for conduct of business to be followed at a meeting including the quorum at the meetings and such other matters in relation to meetings as may be necessary shall be such as may be prescribed by the Statutes.

Powers and duties of Management Council

26. The Management Council shall exercise the following powers and perform the following duties, namely:-

(a) make such provisions, as may enable college and institutions to undertake specialised studies and, where necessary or desirable, organise and make provision for common laboratories, libraries, museums and equipment for teaching and research;

(b) establish departments, colleges, schools, institutions of higher learning, research and specialised studies, hostels and provide housing for staff, on the recommendation of the Academic Council;

(c) make, amend or repeal Ordinances and prepare draft Statutes and make such recommendations thereon to the Senate as it thinks fit;

(d) hold, control and arrange for administration of assets and properties of the university;

(e) present the budget estimates as received from the Finance and Accounts Committee with its own modifications, if any, to the Senate for it final approval;

(f) enter into, vary, carry out and cancel contracts on behalf of the university,

(g) determine the form of a common seal for the university, and provide for its custody and use;

(h) accept, on behalf of the university, trusts, bequests, donations and transfer of any movable or immovable property to the university ;

(i) transfer by sale, or otherwise, any movable property on behalf of the university;

(j) borrow, lend or invest funds on behalf of the university as recommended by the Finance and Accounts Committee;

(k) lay down policy for administering funds at the disposal of the university for specific purpose;

(l) provide buildings, premises, furniture, apparatus and other means needed for conduct of the work of the university.

(m) recommend to the Senate conferment of honorary degrees and academic distinctions;

(n) institute and confer such degrees, diplomas, certificates and other academic distinctions as recommended by the Academic Council and arrange for convocation for conferment of the same, as provided by the Ordinances;

(o) institute fellowships, travelling fellowships, scholarships, studentships, exhibitions, awards, medals and prizes, and prescribe rules therefor in accordance with the Regulations made in this behalf;

(p) make Regulations for collaboration with other universities, institutions and organisations for mutually beneficial academic programmes recommended by the Board of College and University Development;

(q) create posts of university teachers and non-vacation academic staff on the recommendation of the Academic Council as and when required;

(r) lay down by Statute, on the basis of qualifications

and terms and conditions of service and other guidelines approved by the State Government from time to time, and the procedure for appointment of university teachers and non-vocation academic staff and fix their emoluments and norms of workload and conduct and discipline;

(s) create posts of officers and other employees of the university, subject to prior approval of the State Government;

(t) lay down by Statutes the procedures for appointment of officers and other employees of the university, qualifications, mode of recruitment, pay scales, and conditions of service including conduct, discipline and their duties;

(u)prescribe by Statutes procedure for appointment of teachers, officers and other employees in all institutions and colleges affiliated to the university, terms and conditions of their service and rules and procedures for their appointments;

(v) prescribed fees and other charges;

(w) prescribe honoraria, remuneration's and fees travelling and other allowances for paper-setters, examiners and other examination staff, visiting faculty, and for such other services rendered to the university;

(x) receive and consider report of the working of the university from the Vice-Chancellor periodically by the Ordinances;

(y) prepare academic calendar of the university as per the Statutes, and guidelines from the University Grants Commission for next academic year before the expire of the current academic year;

(z) confer autonomous status on university departments, affiliated colleges and recognised institutions on the recommendation of the Academic Council subject to the predetermined norms approved by the State Government having regard to the guidelines of the University Grants Commission.

(aa) consider the perspective plan for the academic development of the university, prepared by the Board of College and University Development;

(bb) assess and approve the feasibility of proposals from the Academic Council for academic programmes;

(cc) consider and adopt the annual report, annual accounts and audit reports and forward them to the Senate for approval;

(dd) cause an inquiry to be made in respect of any matter concerning the proper conduct, working and finances of colleges, institutions or departments of the university;

(ee) delegate, any of its powers except the power to make, amend or repeal Ordinances, to the Vice-Chancellor or such officer or authority of the university or a committee appointed by it, as it thinks fit.

2.6. UNIVERSITY FUNDS, ACCOUNTS AND AUDIT.

Annual financial estimates

27.(1) The annual financial estimates (budget) of the university for ensuing financial year shall be prepared by the Finance and Accounts Officer under the direction of Finance and Accounts Committee, at least two months before the commencement of the financial year.

2. The Finance and Accounts officer shall thereafter forward copies of financial estimates as approved by the Management Council to the Chancellor, Maharashtra State Council for Higher Education and the State Government .

3. The Financial year of the university shall be the same as that of the State Government.

University funds

28. (1) The university shall establish the following funds, namely :-

(a) general fund;

(b) salary fund;

(c) trust fund;

(d) development and programme fund;

(e) contingency fund;

(f) any other fund which, in the opinion of the university, is deemed necessary to establish.

2. The following shall form part of, or be paid into, the general fund,-

(a) non-salary contribution or grant, received from the State Government or Central Government or University Grants Commission;

(b) all incomes of the university from any source whatsoever, including income from fees and charges;

(c) any sum borrowed from the banks or any other agency, with the permission of the State Government ;

(d) sums received from any other source or agency,

3. The salary fund shall consist of all amounts received from the State Government, Central Government or University Grants Commission towards full or part payment of the salary and allowances. No amount from this fund shall be utilised for the purposes other than payment of salary and allowances.

4. All income or money from trusts, bequests,

donations, endowments, subventions and similar grants shall form the trust fund.

5. (a) The development and programme fund of the university shall consists of all infrastructure development grants received from the State Government, all contributions made by the University Grants Commission for development and research grants received from other funding agencies of the Central Government , United Nations and its affiliates, other international agencies, industry, banks and financial institutions or any person;

(b) No amount from this fund shall be appropriated to any other fund of the university or expended for any other purpose;

(c) the development and programme fund shall be utilised in the manner consistent with the object of the programmes for which a suitable code will be adopted to include the guidelines of the funding agency on expenditure and audit, to be granted and approved by the Management Council.

(6) The university shall have and maintain a contingency fund under a separate head of the university accounts which shall be used only for the purpose of meeting any unforeseen expenditure.

(7) Surplus moneys at the credit of these funds, which cannot immediately or at any early date be applied for the purposes aforesaid shall, from time to time, be deposited in the bank as directed by the Management Council.

Table 2.7 : Non-Agricultural Universities in Maharashtra

Sr. No.	*Name of the existing university*	*Name of corresponding University under this Act*	*Universities Area*
	(1)	*(2)*	*(3)*
1.	The University of Bombay, constituted under the Bombay University Act, 1974. (Mah, XXII of 1974)	The University of Bombay.	Districts of (1) City of Bombay (2) Bombay Subrban (3) Raigad (4) Thane (5) Ratnagiri (6) Sindhudurg
2.	The University of Poona, constituted under the Poona Universities Act, 1974 (Mah XXIII of 1974).	The University of Pune	Districts of – (1) Pune (2) Ahmednagar (3) Nashik
3.	The Shivaji University, Constituted under the Shivaji University Act, 1974(Mah XXIV of 1974)	The Shivaji University.	District of (1) Kolhapur (2) Sangli (3) Satara (4) Solapur
4.	The Dr. Babasaheb Ambedkar Marathwada University, constituted under the Marathwada University Act, 1974 (Mah XXX of 1974)	The Dr. Babasaheb Ambedkar Marathwada University.	District of – (1) Aurangabad (2) Jalna (3) Parbhani (4) Nanded (5) Beed (6) Osmanabad (7) Latur
5.	The Nagpur University, constituted under the Nagpur University Act,	The Nagpur University.	District of – (1) Nagpur (2) Bhandara (3) Chandrapur (4) Gadchiroli

	1974(Mah XXVI of 1974).		(5) Wardha.
6.	The Shreemati Nathibai Damodar Thackersey Women's University, constituted under the Shreemati Nathibai Damodar Thackersey Women's University Act, 1974(Mah XXVII of 1974).	The Shreemati Nathibai Damodar Thackersey Women's University.	The State of Maharashtra
7.	The Amaravati University, constituted under the Amaravati University Act, 1983(Mah XXXVII of 1983).	The Amaravati University	Districts of – (1) Amaravati (2) Akola (3) Buldhana (4) Yawatmal
8.	The North Maharashtra University, constituted under the North Maharashtra University Act, 1989(Mah XXIX of 1989)	The North Maharashtra University.	District of – (1) Jalgaon (2) Dhule
9.	The Swammy Ramtirth University, Nanded	The Swammy Ramanand Teerth University, Nanded	(1) Nanded (2) Parbhani (3) Latur

3
Objectives and Methodology

ABSTRACT

In this Chapter details regarding objectives of study, Hypothesis of study, Methodology, data collection sources and limitations of study are discussed. Researcher has visited and studied these universities in Maharashtra for this research. Researcher has also explained the use of MIS with the help of Context Diagram.

3.1. THE PROBLEM TO BE INVESTIGATED

Information is a resource which, like unmined mineral wealth, has no value until extracted, processed and utilised. The management has to adopt various advanced techniques and make use of sophisticated equipments to handle decision making process. As such a well defined and properly implemented Management Information System becomes an essential part of the organisation structure. An ideal MIS can solve half of the problems by itself, leaving only half for the management people.

The 'Management' of any organisation is a

continuous process of problem solving and decision making. 'To Manage' means to have a control, to deal effectively and tactfully with a person. The word 'Management' has got two meanings – first 'an act or, system of managing', second 'a group of people engaged in managing the organisation'. The 'Management' includes every person who gets things done from others and supervisor the actual happenings.

Information plays a vital role in every aspect of management. It is required in planning, organising, leading and controlling. As such one cannot manage the business affairs without Information System. Regardless of the size of the organisation, it is required to have either formal or informal Information System.

Up-till-now few researchers have studied the working of universities in Maharashtra State but the design and development of management Information System has been taken up for the first time. The previous research studies done are mostly belong to the comparison between universities with reference to educational growth, develop and undeveloped geographic area, percentage of literacy etc.

Universities are non- profit making organisations and made for serving the society. The objects of the university shall be to disseminate, create and preserve knowledge and understanding by teaching, research, extension and service and by effective demonstration and influence of its corporate life on society in general

3.2. Objectives of the Study

The main objective of the present study is to evaluate working of selected universities and to develop a suitable computerized MIS model for the university. Other objectives are -

* To provide general view of the University Administration
* To study the administration / operation of selected Universities in Maharashtra State
* To design and develop a functional model of Management Information System for University Administration.
* To Improve efficiency and productivity in staff members of the university.
* To Implement Management Information System in selected sections of the university and carry-out cost benefit analysis.
* To study and evaluate benefits of using MIS in University Administration.
* To provide security measures and authorised access to confidential data / information in database.
* To generate reports (with use of graphs) which will be useful for all the levels of management in university administration.
* To explore the possibilities of applications of MIS to solve the specific problem in University Administration
* To suggest a campus wide Network for implementation of MIS to university

3.3. Sample Selection and Sample Size :

As the collection of data is not possible form each and every university, a few universities were selected. If the data is collected from every member, i.e. universities, the method of collection is called *Census Method* and if the data is collected from a selected few, it is called *Sampling Method.*

Sampling method is based on two principles -

1. Principle of statistical regularity, this principle is based on law of probability.
2. Principle of Inertia of large number, wherein this method states larger the size of the sample wee it is representative of the population

Following are the methods used to select the sample from the population

a) Simple Random Sampling

This method of sampling is subjective in nature, random sampling is a scientific method of selection, which is free form personal bias. Every item has an equal opportunity of being selected in the sample. The following methods are commonly used for random selection.

1. Lottery Method : The method is simple and therefor popular for taking a random sample.

2. Stratified Sampling : Item of each class are included in right proportion in a stratified sample. In order to use this method, we must know what groups, called strata comprise the total population and in what proportion when this is known, items are selected from each stratum proportionately by random method.

Here, Stratified Random Sampling Method was used. In Maharashtra State there are in all total nine universities as mentioned below –

Total Number of Universities in Maharashtra with their year of establishment are

Sr. No.	*Name of University*	*University Area*	*Date of Establishment*
1	University of Mumbai, Mumbai	City of Bombay, Raigad, Thane, Ratnagiri, Sindhudurg	1857
2	University of Nagpur,	Nagpur, Bhandara,	1923

Sr. No.	*Name of University*	*University Area*	*Date of Establishment*
	Nagpur	Chandrapur, Gadchiroli, Wardha	
3	University of Pune, Pune	Pune, Ahmednagar, Nasik	1949
4	The Smt. Nathibai Damodar Thackerscy Women's University, Mumbai	State of Maharashtra	1951
5	Dr. Babasaheb Ambedkar Marathwada University, Aurangabad	Aurangabad, Jalna, Beed, Usmanabad	1958
6	Shivaji University, Kolhapur	Kolhapur, Sangli, Satara, Solapur	1962
7	Amravati University, Amravati	Amravati, Akola, Buldhana, Yavatmal	1983
8	North Maharashtra University, Jalgaon	Jalgaon, Dhule	1991
9	The Swami Ramanand Teerth Marathwada University, Nanded	Nanded, Parbhani, Latur	1995

out of which 30% were selected from the total i.e. 30*9/100 which comes out to be 2.70 i.e. 3 universities were selected by lottery method. They are

1. Pune University, Pune.
2. Shivaji University, Kolhapur.
3. North Maharastra University, Jalgaon

Simple Size : 3

Design and development part of Management Information System is covered as a case study with reference to Shivaji University, Kolhapur.

3.4. Research Methodology of the Study

The present study is based on working of universities in Maharashtra State. As the working of each University differ from each other but all the universities in Maharashtra State come under one act i.e. " The Maharashtra Universities Act. 1994". Thus, keeping in mind the global structure of University administration the Data flow Diagram is made with reference to University Administration. Designing and development part is covered as a case study with reference to Shivaji University, Kolhapur.

The study is based on experimental type of research where researcher mainly intends to develop and ascertain the feasibility of an Management Information System in University Administration. This exercise involves study of the various aspects of university, the organisation structure, operations, functions of the university and managers at all levels of university administration and government policies. Hence methodology adopted and followed with reference to the objectives can be stated as below –

From the objectives it is clear that this study comprises of –

1. Study of existing system with reference to various operations, procedures, organization structure and the state and Central Govt. Policies, UGC Policies.
2. Design and develop an Management Information System for University Administration.

The Data Flow Diagrams will be same to all universities. Data Flow Diagrams are extremely useful in modeling many aspects of a business functions because they systematically subdivide a task into its basic parts, helping the analyst to understand the system that they are trying to model.

A square represents a provider of data (data source) or receiver of data (data since) such as a management. The parallel lines depict a file of data or data store. Arrows show the flow of data of data between the other symbols. Circles stand for a process that converts or transforms data.

Data Flow Diagram Symbols

Squares represent sources (providers) or sinks (receivers) of data

Parallel line represent a data store

Arrow shows data flow

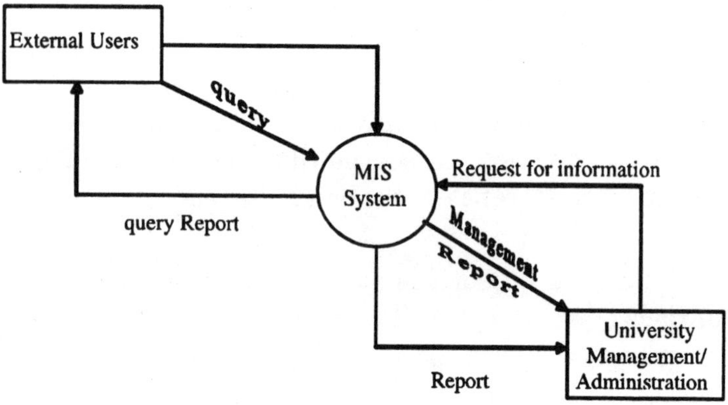

Fig. 3.2. Context Diagram

The Methodology adopted and followed with reference to the objectives of the study is given as under

First of all, in order to review the information system procedures and practices, various reports and relevant information were collected from the office files and records of the selected university. Then the researcher examined the contents of the various reports, periodically, purpose etc. and identified the inter unit and inter-sector differentials.

Then an attempt has been made to evaluate the use of MIS in decision making process. With the help of the views expressed by the top/middle/lower level executives. Interview and personal discussion techniques were used to elicit the view of the executives at different levels.

Then the structures of various databases were finalized and output reports formats were designed.

Finally, conclusions are drawn on the basis of the facts revealed by the study and suggestions are offered keeping in view the problem areas.

3.5. Data Collection Sources

For the present study data is collected through primary as well as secondary sources, this work which attempts to develop a workable prototype Management Information System for University Administration.

Primary Data

a) Data regarding the information system followed by the organisation has been collected by way of personal interviews with the top management and functional heads of the university.

b) Other necessary information is gathered through discussions held with the persons working in various sections / departments and also by observation method.

Secondary Data

The Secondary data includes –

a) Published data collected from various libraries particularly Management Institutes and University form Kolhapur.

b) Various seminars and Research Paper, published and un-published material on Management Information System.

c) Annual Reports, Ledgers, Manuals and Magazines of related work

The data collected from the above source is processed analysed and interpreted and presented in the study.

3.6. Significance of the Study

Management Information means the information required by the management to perform its tasks more efficiently and discharge its responsibilities toward the organisation and its personnel. The information required by the management can be broadly divided into following types-

i. Financial

ii. Costing

iii. Quantitative information regarding Examination, Affiliation etc.

iv. Market

v. Government rules, laws etc.

vi. Research and Development

vii. General

Out of above, the first three types of information are very important in view of the decision making function of the management. As such there is a need to have a properly designed and well implemented information system in the university. Such system will help the management in achieving the university objectives.

Vice-Chancellor of the university looks after the day-to-day administration of the university. Other officers like Pro-Vice-Chancellor, Controller of Examinations, Finance & Accounts Officer, Registrar, and Director, Board of College and University Development assist him.

The researcher visited three universities in Maharashtra State –

* Pune University, Pune.
* North Maharashtra University, Jalgaon.

* Shivaji University, Kolhapur.

The duties and functions of all the universities are uniform in nature. It is an non-profit making organization and all universities in Maharashtra State are come under one act i.e. "The Maharashtra Universities Act, 1994".

The universities are service providers to the society, where the success and credibility largely depends upon the people who work with in the university. The efficient employees are needed to improve the quality and efficiency of university. Therefore, there is a need of continuous research and information cell to monitor the working of these universities.

The present study will definitely help the universities to improve their overall working.

3.7. Its Likely Contribution to Knowledge

The researcher has studied and designed a functional Model of management information system by using a advanced techniques in computer. The researcher has developed a functional model of Management Information System for university administration in Visual Basic – 6 and MS-Access. Which is easily portable on any Personnel Computer or on LAN environment. MIS software has 40 various informative screens with a facility to add, modify, delete, view and print options. It also has a data security provision to avoid unauthorised access to confidential and important data. Various output reports are generated with use of graphs to represent the facts and figures. Which is very user friendly. Any person who has a little knowledge of computer can use this software and extract the information from it. A simple provision is also made to Add, modify or delete the information from database.

Following are the some of the important Reports

generated from MIS developed for University Administration :-

1) List of Colleges affiliated to University
2) List of all Teaching & Non-Teaching Departments
3) List of all equipments, computers install at various sections / Departments of university
4) List of all Budget heads with yearwise provision
5) List of all management Council, Senate, Academic Council members
6) List of all Examiners, Examinations, Examination Centres etc
7) List of all Teaching & Non-Teaching Staff of University
8) List of yearwise convocation reports
9) List of lecture series organised by the university
10) List of all previous Vice-Chancellors and Pro-Vice-Chancellors of the university.

The present study will help the universities to understand and adopt better policies and practices while performing there regular duties by getting a reliable, accurate and speedy information for decision making with minimum man- hours used with less errors.

3.8. Implementation

On-line MIS system has been developed using Visual Basic 6.0 as Front end and MS-Access as a back end tool. All the data is stored in MS-Access. The functional model also works in Multi-user environment.

On-line MIS model has been implemented in two sections of the university namely Convocation section and Budget Section. Required reports are generated using MIS for both sections.

This system has 50 various Screens which accepts and displays the information to the user. Each screen is having facility to add, modify, delete and print, the output reports can be printed or will be displayed on screen. Whenever necessary to represent the figures, researcher has used graphs to represent the facts and figures.

To avoid unauthorized access, MIS system has provided Password as a Security measure. Confidential data/information in data base should not be accessed by an unauthorized user.

4
MIS in University Administration

ABSTRACT

In this chapter the researcher has explained has MIS is useful in University Administration. Researcher has also explained of types of communications in University Administration, Components of MIS in University System Various Advantages of using MIS to top management in University Administration.

4.1. INTRODUCTION

The Management Information System is defined as "A group of people set up manuals and data processing equipments to select, store, process and retrieve data to reduce the uncertainty in decision making by yielding information for managers at the time they can most efficiently use it."

This definition clarifies the role of computers in the information system and decision making process. The "information" part in the system includes any type of data that can be used in effective and efficient decision making process.

In today's complicated business world, management

information system became computerised data processing system, generating reports for various needs and creating database for decision making process.

In any organisation, small or big, major time is spent for data collection, processing, documenting and communicating to concerned people. Major portion of the overheads goes into this type of data collection and processing work in an organisation which is unproductive. All people in organisation are continuously looking for some information which they need to perform their task. Hence, information is people oriented and it varies with the nature of people in the organisation. The difficulty in handling this requirement of the people is on account of a couple of reasons. The information is a processed product fulfilling the imprecise need of the people. It takes time to search data and may require difficult processing path. Unless it is processed and communicated on time, it has no value. The scope and quantum of information is person dependent and it is difficult to conceive information as a well defined product for the entire organisation. Since, people are instrumental to transact business, human error is possible in conducting the business transactions. As human error is difficult to control, the difficulty arises in ensuring hundred percent qualitative information in terms of completeness, accuracy, validity, timelines and meeting the decision making needs.

4.2. MIS and Computer

The role of MIS can be compared with role of heart in the body. Information is the blood and MIS is the heart. The heart plays the role of supplying pure blood to all elements of the body including the brain. The heart works faster when needed to supply more blood. It regulates and controls incoming blood, processes it and sends it to the required destinations. It fulfills all needs of human body in general and also in particular. MIS plays exactly the same role in the organisation. The system ensures that appropriate data is collected from various sources and processed, and sent further to all needy destinations. The system is expected to fulfill the information need of an individuals, group of individuals, management function, managers, and the top management. Since MIS plays a very important role in the organisation, it creates an impact on the organisations functions, performance and productivity.

Translating the real concept of MIS into a reality is technically unfeasible proposition unless computer is used. The computer Hardware and Software is the foundation to Management Information System. MIS depends heavily on Hardware and Software configuration.

The computer system provides security of data, storage of the data on magnetic media in an impersonal mode. The computer system provides facilities such as "Read Only" where you can not delete or update data. Computer helps the authorised person to access the selected information through a scheme of passwords and layout access facility. The confidential nature of data and information can be maintained in the computer system with such facility, MIS becomes a safe application in the organisation.

In computer data processing, once the data has been converted into a machine readable form, the further processing is almost complete automatic as the computer is capable of performing all the data processing functions such as sorting, selecting, summarising, calculating etc. With very little human intervention. This is because the computer has the added capability of storing a series of instructions which infact tells the computer regarding processing and operations of the data.

4.3. Communications in University Administration

Communication may take place through defined organisational network and formal positions. The pattern of communication becomes very complex as university grows in terms of number of departments, colleges and employees. Secondly, formal channels inhibit the free flow of information between different levels. The formal channels may take different forms as shown in following figure

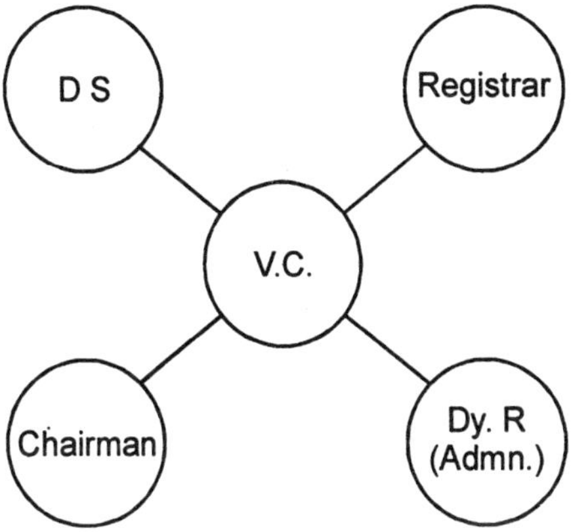

(a) Star

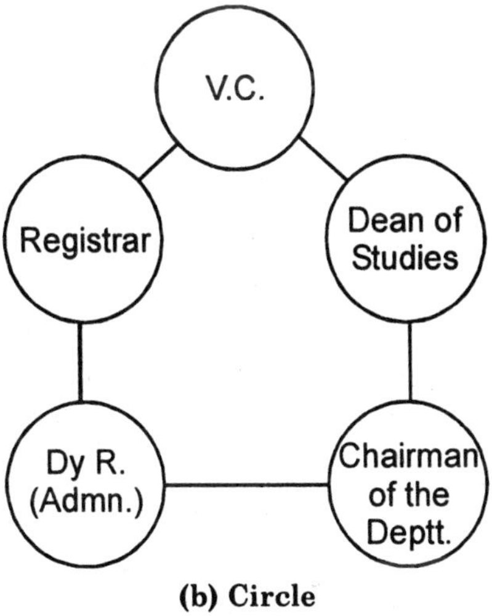

(b) Circle

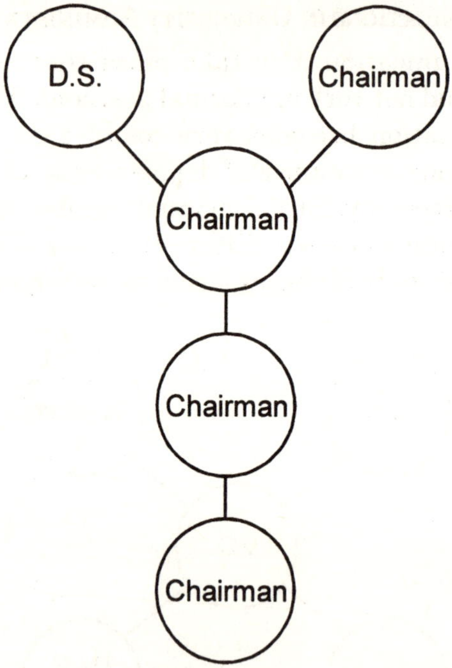

(c) 'Y' Type

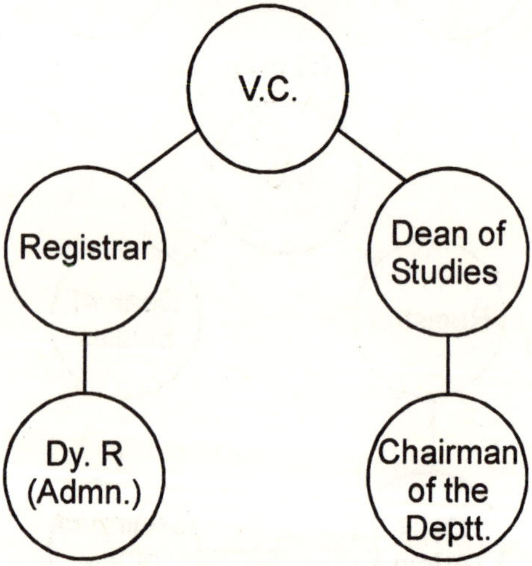

(d) Chain

Fig. 4.1. Types of Communications in University Administration

Let us take an example in which five persons in the university, namely, Vice-Chancellor, Dean of Studies, Chairman of The Department, Registrar, Assistant Registrar (Administration) are required to communicate. The formal communication network may take different forms.

In Circle Network, for example, The Vice-Chancellor can communicate with the Dean of Studies and Registrar. To communicate with Dean of Studies, Registrar will have to go through the Vice-Chancellor or through Assistant Registrar (Administration) and Chairman of the Department. In the star pattern Vice-Chancellor can communicate with Registrar, Dean of Studies, Assistant Registrar(Administration) and Chairman of the Department. But they can not communicate amongst each other.

In another situation of 'Chain', Chairman of the Department could communicate with Assistant Registrar (Administration) through a chain of Dean of Studies, Vice-Chancellor and Registrar. Here the Vice-Chancellor is in the comparatively advantageous situation to control and route communication except interaction between Dean of Studies and Chairman, and Registrar and Assistant Registrar in 'Y' form, whole communication is channeled through Vice-Chancellor except communication between Assistant Registrar (Administration) and Registrar. This is again a centralized network.

4.4. Use of MIS in University Administration

Information is vital to effective management of all undertakings. It is the life blood of business and is playing an ever increasing important role in the day-to-day management and it is becoming a highly valuable business resource both for planning and control.

The prevailing notion that public undertakings

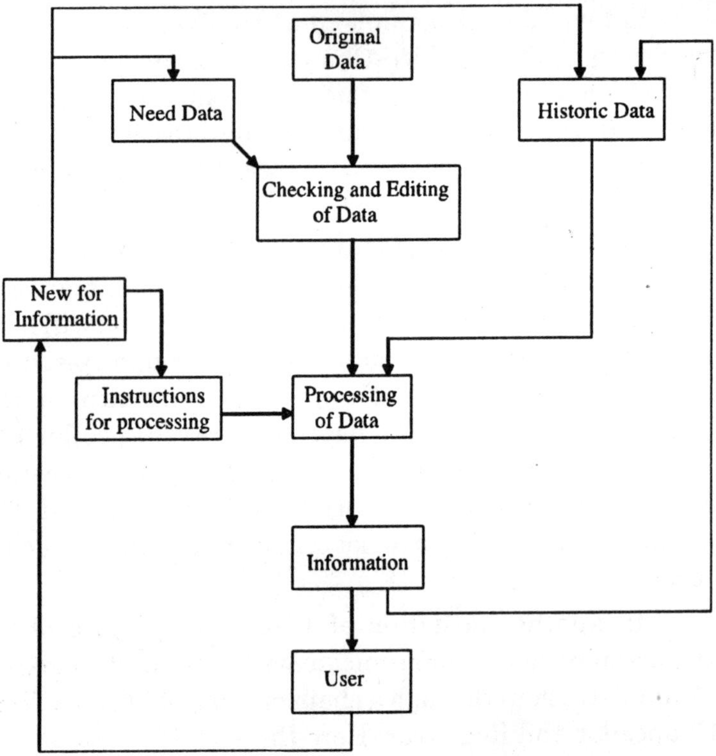

Fig. 4.2. Production of Information

suffer from a surfeit of information is largely true. There is, in general, a plethora of reports and returns which reach various divisions of a public undertaking. Some of these reports often contain information which is duplicated in others. Co-ordination in matter of collection of information and elimination of redundancy are not often realised in practice.

University being considered as Government undertaking is intended to serve help in the following major decision making areas :

1. Support of operational decisions
2. Support of planning or policy decisions

3. Audit and review of Govt. decisions, judicial bodies and outside agencies.

Only MIS can provide proper information to the management. This information will enable to :

1. Measure the impact of decision making before or after they are made.
2. Measure the environment
3. React in an appropriate names in a given time frame learning process to arrive at a meaningful decision.

A brief presentation of different components of MIS is given in following figure

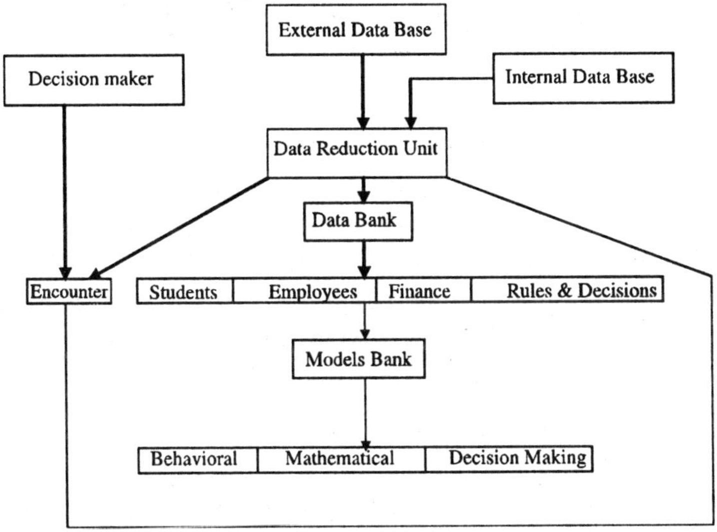

Fig. 4.3. External Data Base

Components of MIS in University System

From the above figure we find that MIS unit will collect different types of information from external as well as from internal sources. Different Systems in the university will ensure continuous flow of information to the MIS. Data reduction unit will engage in screening out irrelevant information. The relevant information will be processed (may not be processed in certain cases) and transferred to different data banks which may be classified in terms of students data bank, employees (teaching and non-teaching separately) data bank, Finance data bank, Rules and decision data bank etc. The real categorisation will depend upon the size and functions of university. Next component is Model-Bank which will include different models which process information and sometimes facilitate decision-making. Whenever, a decision-maker requires information he will approach MIS unit for information. He will validate his own information from the MIS unit and seek tentative solution, this is a simplified schematic presentation of MIS in university.

MIS in the University system may have the following components :

i) Internal Reporting System

Decisions taken at different levels and departments must be communicated to other departments and individuals who may utilise such information in making decisions. An independent MIS unit must have a separate data bank for assembling, recording, processing, storing and retrieving the internal information.

ii) Intelligence

This involves recurrent sensing of the changing societal expectations, employment markets, the government and UGC's policy etc. Information can also be available on different aspects of university administration collected from other similarly situated universities.

iii) Research

MIS must contain information about the attitudes, beliefs and expectations of different sections of the university, popularly known as multiple masters. For such information, survey research may be required. Similarly, for knowing the level of job-satisfaction and morale, effectiveness of leadership styles, certain research may be essential.

4.5. Advantages of Using MIS in the University Administration

With the use of Management Information System (MIS) in University administration, all the sections will be connected to each other by which they can share the information and arrive at optimal decisions in limited time. The Top Management authorities will get on-line up-to-date information before taking any decisions.

A) Hon. Vice Chancellor & Hon. Pro Vice Chancellor

Hon. Vice Chancellor has to take decisions on four major areas of university administration i.e. Examination, Finance, College affiliation and general administration. Every day hundreds of folders from various sections come to Hon. Vice-chancellor's office for decision. Hon. V.C. has to read all the folders and concern officers remarks and then he has to give his final decision, before taking the decision he needs a up-to-date correct information.

If MIS is available to Hon. Vice Chancellor, then before giving any decision with use of MIS system, he can check by himself and verify the facts mentioned in folders of any section, e.g.

Management / User can get information regarding Examination section through MIS as -

1. What is the schedule of next examination
2. How many paper setters are to be appointed
3. How many subjects / courses are run by university
4. How many examiners are registered to subjectwise for paper checking/practical examination

5. How many labs are available for practical examination subjectwise/college wise etc
6. How many Centres will conduct the examination
7. How many students are going to appear for various examinations
8. Total non-teaching staff available in various exam sections total temporary staff appointed.
9. List of Directors appointed for various Central Assessment centres.
10. Convocation details
11. List of scholarships, awards to various students/ colleges
12. College wise seating capacity for conducting examinations.

Management / User can get information regarding Finance section through MIS as :

1. List of all Budget Heads and the provision for particular year
2. Up-to-date expenditure done in each budget head with exact balance available
3. How many grants received by various funding agency
4. How many grants are pending with various funding agency
5. Balance of various bank accounts and Fixed Deposit accounts
6. Total salary expenditure on Teaching and Non-teaching staff cadre wise and section wise
7. Total overtime given to employees
8. Amount spent on conducting examinations and money received for examinations by way of various examination fees.

9. Total Travelling Allowance given to staff
10. Various taxes paid by university to Govt. agency like Income tax, Professional tax etc.
11. Total of purchasing of various items recurring/non-recurring
12. Total fixed assets and liabilities
13. Balance sheet and other documents of various years
14. Information regarding Self Supporting Schemas.

Management / User can get information regarding Affiliation section through MIS as :

1. List of all Affiliated colleges to university
2. Type of affiliation, last date of temp. affiliation, Name and address of Principals
3. Sex wise/class wise/category wise number of students at various colleges
4. Various courses/subjects taught at various colleges
5. List of college teachers with other details like qualification, specialisation, teaching experience, date of retirement, address, etc.
6. Fees deposited/pending with colleges
7. Court matter status regarding various colleges/staff
8. List of all colleges Principals with address and phone/fax numbers

Management / User can get information regarding Administration section through MIS as -

1. List of all Teaching and Non-teaching employees with other details like date of joining, qualification, address, phone numbers, service record, leave record, present section, awards received, blood group, etc.
2. List of all Management Council members, Academic Council Members with address and phone numbers

3. List of all retired employees
4. Section wise list of employees
5. List of students staying in hostels
6. List of all court matters cases pending with various courts
7. University campus security system details
8. List of all V.I.P. guests with address
9. List of all University vehicles details like date of purchase, cost, registration number, insurance, make, chassis number, engine number, etc
10. Information regarding Annual Report, Seminar, Lecture Series, Scholarship and prizes.
11. Insurance record for all university equipments and fixed assets

Management / User can get information regarding various Teaching Departments through MIS as -

* Name of Department
* Name of Head of department
* Names of various courses run at department
* Sex/cast wise number of students at department
* Teaching staff at departments with qualification, Specialisation, experience etc.
* Non Teaching staff at department
* Equipments / Computers at department
* Books at department library
* Number of class rooms and seating capacity
* Built-up area of Department (in Sq.ft.)
* List of conferences, workshops and seminars conducted by each department.
* List of Research Publications / Articles in various National and International Journals of each faculty

and departments.

Management/User can get information regarding Library through MIS as

* Number of Books at library (subject wise)
* Number of periodicals/journals at library
* Year wise expenditure on books
* Teaching staff at library
* Non Teaching staff at library
* Equipments / Computers at library
* Built-up area of Library (in Sq.ft.)
* Budget provision for library (yearwise)

Management / User can get information regarding University Press, Computer Centre, Health Centre, University Scientific Instrumentation Centre (USIC), Common Facility Centre (CFC) through MIS as -

* List of equipments with cost, year of purchase etc. :
* Technical staff
* Non Technical staff
* Activities performed
* Income generated by rendering services to outside agencies/departments

B) Hon. Registrar needs following information before taking any decision

1. List of all Teaching and Non-teaching employees with other details like date of joining, qualification, address, Phone no., service record, leave record, present section, awards received, blood group, etc.
2. List of all retired employees
3. Section wise list of employees
4. List of students staying in hostels

5. List of all court matters cases pending with various courts
6. University campus security system details
7. List of all V.I.P. guests with address
8. List of all University vehicles details like date of purchase, cost, registration number, insurance, make, chassis number, engine number, etc
9. Information regarding Annual Report, Seminar, Lecture Series, Scholarship and prizes.

C) Hon. Controller of Examinations needs following information before taking any decision

1. What is the schedule of next examination
2. How many paper setters are to be appointed
3. How many subjects / courses are run by university
4. Entrance test merit list and Admission chart, Course and college wise
5. How many examiners to be called subjectwise for paper checking/practical examination
6. How many labs are available for practical examination subjectwise/college wise etc.
7. How many Centres will conduct the examination
8. How many students are going to appear for various examinations
9. Total non-teaching staff available in various exam sections total temporary staff appointed.
10. List of Directors appointed for various Central Assessment centres.
11. Convocation details
12. List of scholarships, awards to various students/ colleges.

D) Hon. Finance & Accounts Officer needs following information before taking any decision

1. List of all Budget Heads and the provision for particular year
2. Up-to-date expenditure done in each budget head with exact balance available
3. How many grants received by various funding agency
4. How many grants are pending with various funding agency
5. Balance of various bank accounts and Fixed Deposit accounts
6. Total salary expenditure on Teaching and Non-teaching staff on cadre wise and section wise
7. Total overtime given to employees
8. Amount spend on conducting examinations and money received for examination by way of collecting various examination fees.
9. Total Travelling Allowance given to staff
10. Various taxes paid by university to Govt. agency like Income tax, Professional tax etc.
11. Total of purchasing of various items recurring/non-recurring
12. Total fixed assets and liabilities
13. Balance sheet and other documents of various years
14. Information regarding Self Supporting Schemes.

E) Hon. Director, Board of College & University Development needs following information before taking any decision

1. List of all Affiliated colleges to university
2. Type of affiliation, last date of temp. affiliation, Name and address of Principals

3. Sex wise/class wise/category wise number of students at various colleges
4. Various courses/subjects taught at various colleges
5. List of college teachers with other details like qualification, specialisation, teaching experience, date of retirement, address, etc.
6. Fees deposited/pending with colleges
7. Court matter status regarding various colleges/staff

5
Designing the Data Structure

ABSTRACT

This chapter covers four phases of System Analysis and Design namely System Analysis

* *Scope and Objective of New System*

System Design

* *Model of the New System DFD and ERD*
* *Develop a Method for Collecting Data*
* *Data Dictionary*
* *Program Specifications*

System Implementations

* *Writing testing a documenting programs*
* *System Maintenance*

5.1. PHASE- I : SYSTEMS ANALYSIS

Systems projects involve a sequence of phases called a systems life cycle which consists of four distinct phases–

* Analysis
* Design
* Implementation

* Maintenance

System Analysis : Involves studying the ways an organization currently retrieves and process data to produce information with the goal of determining how to make it work better. To do so, the Systems Analyst may develop alternative systems and evaluate each in terms of cost / benefit and feasibility.

Systems Design : Requires the analyst to decide on the formats of the reports that the system will produce, define data-storage methods, plan how to collect and input data, and define the necessary programs. Design is the second phase in the systems life cycle.

Systems Implementation : Includes actual programming, testing, training and use of the new system. Upon completion of the system, the analyst, users, and management evaluate the system to ensure that it fulfills all its goals. Implementation is the third phase of the systems process.

System Maintenance : System maintenance includes repairing the system when errors are detected, enhancing the system when the user needs new functions, or changing the system to meet new laws or changes in the organization's purpose of goals.

System life Cycle

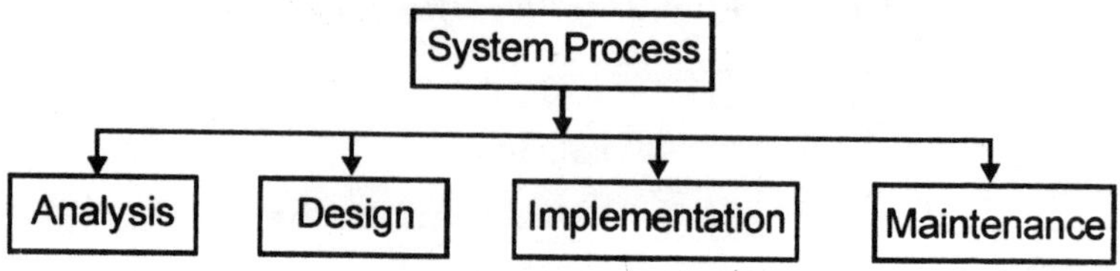

Fig. 5.1

Systems analysis includes both a preliminary and a detailed stage. During preliminary analysis, the analyst takes a quick look at what is wanted and whether its costs and benefits justify the perceived want. Detailed analysis includes an in-depth look at what is wanted and contains more refined cost and benefit studies.

The Preliminary analysis stage begins when someone perceives a problem, desires a modification to an existing system, needs a repair to an existing system, or demands an entirely new system.

The report that results from the detailed analysis becomes a document called a feasibility study or a requirements document. This report further expands the systems study, in far greater detail-

* Problem definition
* Scope and objectives of a "new" system
* Alternative solutions.
* Cost benefit analysis derived from alternatives.
* Potential organizational or policy changes.
* Description of the out puts of the new system.
* System Development and Redevelopment Process

5.1.1. Problem Definition

Management Information System for University administration is online information system to the top management in the university which assist them in decision making by providing accurate, timely are reliable information.

Other users can also use same Management Information System to update their knowledge on various sections of the university. Which saves the time and money.

5.1.2. Scope and objectives of New System

To provide the accurate, reliable and timely information for decision making in university administration as well as to the external user. Summary

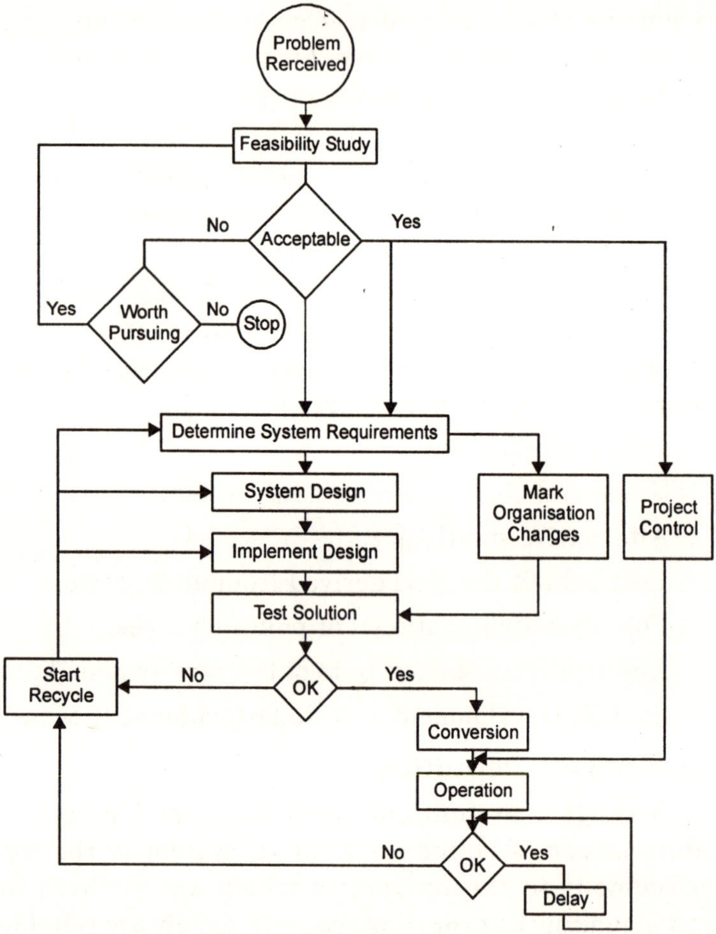

Fig. 5.2

reports on various sections of university and few reports are with use of graphs for better understanding and comparison between more than one variable are provided in the new system.

Information required either to the External or Internal user at any time without wasting his time and money is the major objective of this system. Only authorised user will have an access to the related databases and permissions to modify or delete the data stored in database.

5.1.3. Cost and Benefit Analysis

Due to use of computers we have the benefit of searching, ease in calculations, clarity, facility to generate various types of report demanded by the management. Jobs can be process repeatedly. With use of computers, data security can also be provided.

Due to use of MIS for University Administration following Benefits will be availed by the university Management

1. With less manpower, speedy availability of information for decisions making is possible due to use of computers and MIS.
2. Reports to be submitted to Central Govt., State Govt. and UGC are to be submitted on urgent basis from various sections and in various formats. Same reports can be generated through MIS within very limited time with more accuracy and reliability.
3. Concept of 'Paper less Office' can be adopted by the authorities with use of Intranet throughout campus. This concept of Paper less office is adopted by Agricultural University, Parbhani in May 2001.
4. Maintenance of huge old record like ledgers and files can be avoided because all data/Information can be stored on computer it self and can be extracted as and when required.
5. Office work can be managed with less space.
6. As data/Information is stored at MIS server centrally redundancy of data can be avoided.
7. Source code of the MIS software with the university, Therefore any modification or addition in software can be incorporated very easily and without any charges.

8. There will not be any dependency on outside party to maintain the software which saves the money and time.
9. Existing hardware like printers, and PC's can be used in proposed network, which saves hardware cost.
10. Instead of sending hard copy, reports can be send through electronic media like Floppy or Compact Disk, which saves postage charges.
11. As the data is in electronic format, same can be send through Internet to any corner of the world with less time and very little cost.
12. Non confidential information can be made open to all, so that general public can also access the information they required by providing separate node at enquiry counter which saves the time of public and University staff to provide such information.
13. Any information required by the Management Council, Academic Council and Senate member while meeting is proceeding can be available immediately, so that discussion and decision can be taken in the same meeting instead of postponing the same for next meeting.
14. Research students can get the data related to university on various areas like finance, examination etc centrally at one server so their time in collecting same data can be avoided.
15. Most of the State and Central Government offices are computerised. Therefore they are also giving / demanding the information to the universities in electronic media.
16. Cost of the hardware is reducing day-by-day but appointment of new staff is like adding more

overheads to the financial liability of the University.

17. As globalisation and open market concept is spreading in India, Foreign Universities will come to India with all modern infrastructure and for their competition our Universities have to adopt advanced technology as early as possible.
18. As per the survey it is found that one PC and a operator can perform the duties of Five Persons to complete same job manually.
19. Important record of the university has to be preserve for atleast 40 years and keeping records in files for 40 years is very difficult but is very easy on computer where year wise information can be compressed and kept on CD's and can be extracted as and when required by putting same CD again into the computer, which saves time and cost of maintenance of old record.
20. With use of scanners old record which is at present is in files and folder can be converted to electronic media and can be stored permanently on computer.
21. In near future all the affiliated colleges / University will be connected to each other and official correspondence from the colleges to the University and Vice-Versa will be possible through computer, which also saves time and postage cost. Therefore, computerization of University Administration is must at University level.
22. Last two years there has been ban on new appointment of staff by the State and Central Government, many posts are vacant and due to this work load has been increased on present staff. The Administration work has to be completed in time, therefore, use of computer and MIS is the only tool

available with the University Management to complete the work in time with less manpower.

23. Due to MIS, before taking any decision, top management can check the facts mentioned in the folder with actual information available on MIS and then only it will be easy to take right decision at right time.

5.1.4. Description of the new systems major outputs

For any University administration, major output reports required are -

* On line help for each major sections
* Easy facility to add / modify / delete the information from data base
* Hard copy of report in various formats
* Reports with use of graphs for easy comparison between two or more variables among the information
* Security measures to access and modify confidential information
* Restricted access to external users

5.2. Phase – II : Systems Design

After decision-makers and the user have approved the required documents, then the analyst begins the second step in the system life-cycle ; Systems Design. During this phase, the analyst schedules design activities, works with the user to determine the various data inputs to the system, plans how data will flow through the system, design required for outputs and writes program specifications. Again, the analyst's activities focus on solving a user's problem in logical terms.

During this second step, analysts employ a variety of tools such as data flow diagrams, entity-relationship diagrams, data dictionaries (lists of terms and their definitions) and the Gantt chart (a graph depicting design events, personnel assignment, and time schedules).

A new tool, prototyping software, has evolved recently. Prototyping software allows the analyst to generate quickly an initial version of the system for the user to review. The prototyping software includes facilities that automatically generate. Screens, printed reports, and essential logic functions for collecting and storing data, essentially, the user and the analyst use prototyping to experiment with the new system, prototyping enables the analyst to move quickly from a preliminary logical design for the system to a physical realization of that design. After experimenting with the prototype, changes are made to the original logical design, which is then re-prototyped. This prototype-review-change process continues until the user and the analyst are both satisfied with the system's design. The systems design converts the theoretical solution introduced by the feasibility study into a logical reality.

5.2.1. Model of the new system -

Data modeling, through the use of entity-relationship diagrams (ERD's) and process modeling, through Data Flow Diagrams (DFD's) are techniques that help analysts study the information structure of a business function. Using these techniques analysts can better understand the business functions in detail. Once the data and process models of a business functions are captured on paper, they can guide the design of a new computer-based system to support that business function.

5.2.1.1. Data Flow Diagram

Depict how data interact with a system some professionals call them data flow graphs, or bubble charts. Whatever they're called, data flow diagrams are extremely useful in modeling many aspects of a business function because they systematically subdivide a task into its basic parts, helping the analyst to understand the system that they are trying to model.

A square represents a provider of data (data source) or receiver of data (data sink), such as a property holder or management. The parallel lines depict a file of data or data store;

This DFD notation is often referred to as 'Yordon / De macro' notation. Another widely used DFD notation is called 'Gane / Sarson'. DFD's is that the rectangles with rounded corners for process, rather than circles. Yourdon / Demacro uses parallel lines for a data store while Gane / Sarson uses and open-ended rectangle.

Squares, parallel line, and circles receive names. Arrows also receive names, except when they point to or from a data store file. Some data flow diagram authors also name the data flow to or from a data store, especially when the data flow uses only part of the data held by the data store

Symbols of Data flow Diagrams

Squares represent sources (providers) or sinks (receives) of data

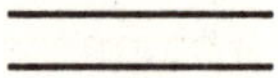

Parallel lines represent a data store

Arrow show data flows.

Circles give processes.

We start all data flow diagrams by drawing the context diagram. This diagram displays "a big picture" of the system under scrutiny. It shows the system at an overview level. The context diagram defines the boundary of the system, it identifies the participants. This is a very important step in the concept of modeling because it specifies what the system under study is and what is its interface with other systems out side the model. Context diagram is so simple that even people unfamiliar with computers or the technical user of data flow diagrams can easily understand it.

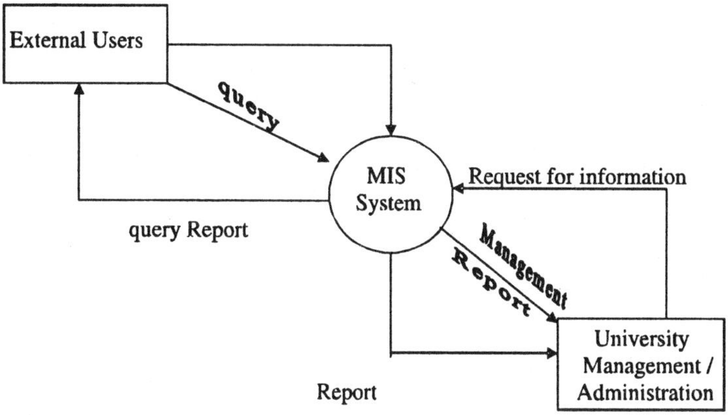

Fig. 5.3. Context Diagram

5.2.1.2. Entity-Relationship Diagram

The term entity is very broadly defined as an object or event that is of interest to the business function that we are trying to model. It is real and has data content associated with it. An entity itself does not convey or contain any data. The data resides in the attributes of the entity. Attributes are the characteristics or properties that describe an entity or describe what we want to store for this entity. An attribute corresponds to a field in a record. The entities are connected by relationships.

For example entity type EXAMINER contains the following attributes

Field	*Field Name*	*Type*	*Data Size*
1.	NAME	Text	40
2.	NAME_EXAM	Text	40
3.	EXAM_SEX	Text	1

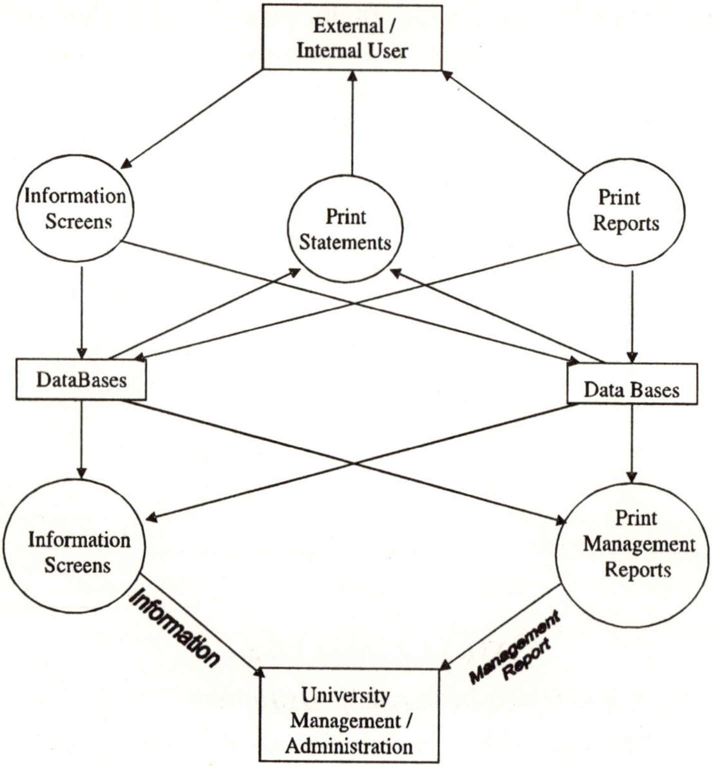

Fig. 5.4. Level – I – DFD

4.	NAME_SUBJ	Text	30
5.	EXAM_ADD1	Text	50
6.	EXAM_ADD2	Text	50
7.	EXAM_ADD3	Text	50
8.	EXAM_PHONE	Text	10
9.	EXAM_TEACH_PG	Long Integer	4
10.	EXAM_TEACH_GR	Long Integer	4
11.	EXAM_QUIF	Text	20
12.	COLG_CODE	Long Integer	4

The attributes of EXAMINER in the above table are technically attribute types, and are the names of the things

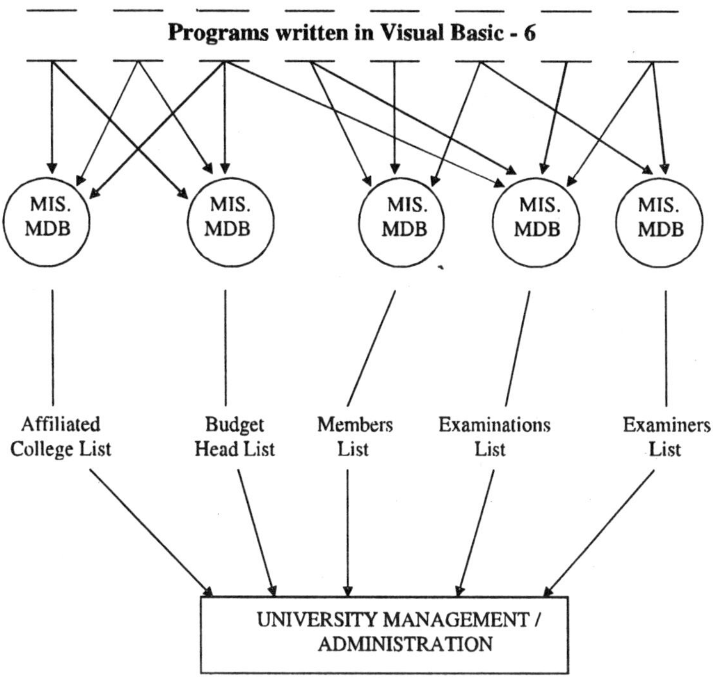

Fig. 5.5. Level – 2 DFD of Print Reports

that we would use to describe the entity EXAMINER. When we give actual data values to there attributes types, we have a set of attribute types that describe a specific entity instance of examiner. The below table shows one instance of EXAMINER

Field	*Field Name*	*Instance*
1	NAME	PATIL SHIVAJI RAJARAM
2	NAME-EXAM	B.SC; M.SC
3	EXAM-SEX	M
4	NAME-SUBJ	BOTANY
5	EXAM-ADD1	PLOT NO 123
6	EXAM-ADD2	STATE BANK COLONY
7	EXAM-ADD3	KOLHAPUR-410020
8	EXAM-PHONE	662560

9	EXAM-TEACH-PG	08
10	EXAM-TEACH-GR	12
11	EXAM-QUIF	M.Sc, Ph.D.
12	COLL-CODE	NCK

It is very important to realize that the data model we constructed here is purely logical- it is part of the 'blueprint' of the underlying information structure of order entry. Nothing in the data model or in the attribute description says anything about what kind of computer contains this data. Whether the files are sequential, indexed or direct, where the stored information physically resides, or whether we have a centralized or distributed databases. At this point the model is a logical-not a physical.

5.2.3. Formats for All the reports that the System will Generate

System design transform a logical representation of what a given system is required to do into the physical specifications. The specifications are converted into a physical reality during development. The design forms a blueprint of the system and how the components relate to each other.

The design phase proceeds according to an orderly sequence of steps, beginning with review and assignment of tasks and ending with package design. During the first stage, output design, an analyst determines what data the application produces and how to organize and present that data. The following guidelines apply to any report –

* The information should be clear and accurate, yet concise, and restricted to relevant data
* Reports should have titles, the date, descriptive heading for columns of data, numbered page and so on. If printed, they should also appear or a standard size of paper

* The reports contents should be in a logical arrangement so that users can easily locate what they need
* The report should come on an output medium that best suits the user's needs

Reports fall into two broad Categories – Internal and External. Managers and other decision makers within an organisation use internal reports to track performance, External reports circulate among customers, Govt. agencies etc.

Most of the reports contain all or some of the following design elements: report heading, page heading, control heading, column heading, detail line, control footing, page footing and report footing. These design elements serve two purposes; they make the report easier to read and they provide a way to control the content of the report.

After thoroughly considering reports eventual use, an analyst will decide which of the design elements to include in it.

Most organizations find that they use a mixture of file types of reports- query, detail, summary, exception, and periodic. Although most conform to basic formatting requirements, each has a unique purpose and audience that dictate special format considerations.

5.2.4. Develop a Method for collecting and / or Inputting Data

All the data related to the University administration is required to be enter in a computer designed forms. 50 various Screens are designed to add, modify the data in various tables in an data base.

A control system is a set of procedures that ensures proper and approved system operation. Verification and Validation during data collection and entry, time stamping (dating), page numbering of printed reports, and basic security provisions such as passwords, read and write access to files, and file backups. A control system helps to prevent computer related fraud and can reduce errors. Once and error enters a computerized system, it takes a lot of time and money to remove it.

The analyst can build controls into a system at the input, processing or at output stages. Controls are costly because they not only demand extra effort by the data entry staff during input, but they consume valuable computer time during processing or output. In the long run, however, the costs of good controls out weigh the costs of errors.

Control System fall into two broad categories – Machine and manual. A computer based (machine) control system uses the computer to help detect errors with a manual control system, someone visually checks for errors. Quite often, combinations of machine and manual control systems make sense.

After an organization has collected, verified, validated and processed its data, it wants to produce output, usually in the form of reports.

Data enters an organizations information system from both internal and external sources. Internal data, from employees and management. External data comes from people and agencies outside the organization.

After pinpointing the data sources, an analyst determines the method of data entry. Manual data entry requires that someone use a terminal or personal computer to key the data. Each of these devices, as their names imply, stores data in different media, usually Floppy disk or Hard disks.

5.2.5. Detailed data requirements with a data dictionary

Regardless of an organization's size of the particular application in question, an analyst will set up seven kinds of files : master, transaction, back up, temporary, suspense, table, and program.

A master file stores all the permanent semi permanent data relevant to a particular application until that data grow obsolete. Transaction, or detail files held data describing the details of a business activity. Back up files provide copies of other files, thus ensuring data replacement in the event of loss, theft or sabotage. Organization usually store back up files on tapes. Suspense files record errors detected by validation programs. Table files held infrequently changing tabular data. These types of files typically provide the necessary data that a program needs for computation or reference. Program files, as the name implies, store the source language programs needed to operate the system.

Normalization

Once the analyst finishes deciding on the various tables, indexes and attributes, yet another step remains normalization. A set of design criteria and five rules, normalization helps data base designers prove that their logical design is correct and optimal. Normalization is the idea that as each of the five rules is applied, undesirable features are removed from the design.

Each successive rule implies that the prior ones are met e.g. of the design meets the third rule or third normal form (often abbreviated 3NF), it should have already met 1NF and 2NF. Normalization implies splitting tables (relations) into two or more tables with fewer columns. Most design try to reach 3NF and a few 4NF, but not many reach 5NF (or need to). The five normalization rules are –

1NF. Each row or column must have a single value with no repeating values

2NF. Every non key column must depend on the primary key

3NF. No non key column can depend on another non key column

4NF. An entity can not have a 1: N relationship between primary key columns and non key columns

5NF. Bread all tables into the smallest possible pieces to eliminate all redundancy with in a table

Batch processing

In a batch processing environment, the organization collects data over a period of time, then processes them in groups at specified intervals. The main advantage of batch processing is its simplicity and relatively low cost.

Online Processing

In an on-line processing environment, users with their terminals can inquire about data at any time other than during updation of their data. User can update data by changing existing – as well as adding new and deleting old information. Online systems are more sophisticated and complex. Each record is processed immediately when it enters into the system.

Local Area Network (LAN)

One of the easiest types of networks is the local area Network (LAN). Most LAN's area take-off on the bus topology. LAN's link PC's together within a limited but geographically shared area, typically within 2000 meters. The heart of the LAN is a server, usually a dedicated device that allows PCs to share another device. A printer server permits the sharing of printers, a file server shares disk or tape storage facilities

For the present study detail Hardware and Software requirement with campus wide network diagram is suggested in chapter no. 8.

5.2.6. Program Specifications

Having defined programs, structures, programming language, the analyst gathers together the outputs from all the other phases of the design activities to form the program specifications. Program specifications take the form of report with the following elements –

i. System

ii. Program Name

iii. Analyst & Programmer

iv. Background

v. Database Layout

vi. Input Data

vii. Processing Requirements

viii. Output Reports

5.3. Phase – III Systems Implementation

During the implementation phase, the system actually takes physical shape. As in the other two stages, the analyst, his or her associates, and the user perform many tasks, including –

* Writing, testing, debugging and documenting programs
* Training the system's users
* Developing operating procedures for the computer center staff

The analyst's involvement in each of these activities

Table 5.1 : Data Dictionary

Sr. No.	*Data Element Name*	*Data Type & Width*	*Item Description*	*Tables used*
1	Exam_Year	C,4	Examination Year	Admission, Prize, Result.
2	Exam_Code	N,4	Examination Code	Admission, Examination, Prize, Exam Schedule, Result, Student Result, Students
3	Colg_Code	N,4	College Code	Admission, Affiliated-College, Examiners, Members, Students
4	Cent_Code	N,4	Centre Code	Affiliated _Colleges
5	Bud_Year	C,9	Budget Year	Budget
6	Bud_Code	C,4	Budget Code	Budget, Budget Mst.
7	Dept_Code	N,4	Department Code	Computers Campus, Departments, Dept. Details, Equipment's
8	Fac_Code	N,4	Faculty Code	Convocation Details, Courses, Examinations
9	Stud_Prn	C,10	Student Permanent Registration Number	Prize, Students
10	Desg_Code	N,5	Designation Code	Staff
11	Subject_Code	N,4	Subject Code	Students
12	Course_Type	N,4	Course Type	Courses
13	Exam_Fee	N,8	Examination Fee	Admission
14	Conv_Year	N,4	Convocation Year	Convocation Details
15	Total_Colg	N,4	Total Colleges	Examination, Faculty

varies from organization to organization. For a small organization, the analyst may perform all the phases and tasks. In large organizations, specialists may work on different phases and tasks, such as training, ordering hardware, converting data from old system to the new.

The implementation phase ends with an evaluation of the system after placing it into operation for a period of time. To make sure that the system performs as expected, however, a final system audit or review takes place. The system audit is a last check or review of a system to ensure that it meets design criteria. Evaluation forms the feedback part of the cycle that keeps implementation going as long as the system continues in operation.

5.3.1. Writing, Testing and Documenting Programs

The present software is written in Visual Basic-6 as a front end tool and output reports are generated with Crystal Report 7. All the data is store in MS-Access as a backend.

The server should be Pentium III with 20 GB Hard Disks and any number of nodes may be attached, which may or may not have Disk. Two Dot matrix printers are advised for printing reports.

The same may be tested on a stand alone machine. Recommended Configuration is as follows –

PC - 486 and above

1.44 MB FDD, CD ROM Drive

20 GB and above HDD

1 Dot matrix printer

Here, the software is available on a CD Drive which may be installed on any machine simply by executing –

setup.exe

All the files from the CD will be copied in C:\ MIS directory. The Setup procedure will create an MIS icon on Program Menu of Windows-98. User has to click same MIS icon to enter in On-line MIS. The MIS system will ask User Name and Password. User should give user name as 'mis' and password as 'mis'.

The PC should have Visual Basic-6, MS-Access and Crystal Report-7 on machine before executing setup.exe, MIS. Mdb is having data base files in MS-Access formats.

5.4. Phase-IV System Maintenance

Software development work never seems to end, users almost always want changes or encounter problems. Thus, the systems maintenance part of the systems process deserves special attention. It is during systems maintenance that the analyst:

* Resolves necessary changes
* Corrects errors
* Enhances or modifies the system
* Assigns staff to perform maintenance activities
* Provides for scheduled maintenance

Most systems spend the bulk of their time in the maintenance phase, with constant enhancements and repairs. Studies show that more money is spent in this fourth phase than in all of the others combined. Writing systems that require as little maintenance as possible is one of the primary goals, as well as one of the benefits of today's modern methodology of software development.

6
Implementation and Reports

ABSTRACT

This chapter covers the structures of the various files used in the present system and various screens and reports generated from the system. This MIS System is developed in Visual Basic – 6, Access and in Crystal Report. This covers Approx. 40 Various informative screens and various output reports.

6.1. FILE STRUCTURES

The present topic lists the structures of the various files used in the present study. The structures are as follows-

Table 6.1

Structures No.	*Table of structure*
6.1.1	Computers on Campus
6.1.2	Designation
6.1.3	Departments
6.1.4	Equipments
6.1.5	Lecture Series
6.1.6	Library

6.1. Screens

The present topic lists all the screens developed to add, modify delete the information in MIS for university administration-

Structures No.	*Table of structure*
6.1	Security Screens
6.2	Main Menu
6.2.1	General Administration
6.2.2	Examination
6.2.3	Finance & Account
6.2.4	Director BCUD
6.2.5	General Information
6.2.1.1	Computer on Campus
6.2.1.2	Designation
6.2.1.3	Departments
6.2.1.3(a)	Departments
6.2.1.4	Equipments
6.2.1.5	Lecture Series
6.2.1.6	Library
6.2.1.7	Members
6.2.1.8	Phone Number
6.2.1.9	Schemes
6.2.1.10	Staff
6.2.1.10(a)	Staff
6.2.1.11	Legal Section
6.2.1.12	Vehicles
6.2.2.1	Faculty
6.2.2.2	Courses
6.2.2.3	Examinations
6.2.2.4	Examination Centers
6.2.2.5	Subjects
6.2.2.6	Admission
6.2.2.7	Students
6.2.2.8	Examination Schedule
6.2.2.9	Examiners
6.2.2.10	Results
6.2.2.11	Prizes
6.2.2.12	Convocation

6.2.2.13	Central Assessment Centre
6.2.3.1	Annual Maintenance Contract
6.2.3.2	Budget
6.2.3.3	Payment
6.2.3.4	Bank Deposits
6.2.3.5	Income Tax
6.2.3.6	Rate Contract
6.2.4.1	Affiliated Colleges
6.2.4.2	Research Work
6.2.4.3	College / University Teachers
6.2.5.2	University Organisation Charts
6.2.5.2(a)	1) Registrar
6.2.5.2(b)	2) Controller of Examination
6.2.5.2(c)	3) Finance of Accounts officer
6.2.5.2(d)	4) Director BCUD
6.2.5.3	Awards
6.2.5.4	Universities
6.2.5.5	VC / PVC History
6.2.5.6	Guest Information

6.3. Output Reports

The present topic lists the various output reports generated by the system.

Structures No.	*Title of Report*
6.3.1	Computer on Campus
6.3.2	Designation List
6.3.3	Departments List
6.3.4	Equipments List
6.3.5	Lecture Series List
6.3.6	Library Information
6.3.7	Members List
6.3.8	Phone Number List
6.3.9	Schemes List
6.3.10	Staff Information

6.3.11	Legal Section Information
6.3.12	Vehicles Information
6.3.13	Faculty List
6.3.14	Courses Information
6.3.15	Examinations List
6.3.16	Examination Centers List
6.3.17	Subjects List
6.3.18	College wise Admission Information
6.3.19	College wise Students List
6.3.20	Examination Schedule
6.3.21	Examiners List
6.3.22.1	Results Report - 1
6.3.22.2	Results Report - 2
6.3.23	Prizes List
6.3.24.1	Convocation Report - 1
6.3.24.2	Convocation Report - 2
6.3.25	Central Assessment Information
6.3.26	Annual Maintenance Contract Report
6.3.27	Budget Report
6.3.28.1	Payment Report - 1
6.3.28.2	Payment Report - 2
6.3.29	Bank Deposit Report
6.3.30	Income Tax Information
6.3.31	Rate Contract Information
6.3.32	Affiliated Colleges List
6.3.33	Research work Information
6.3.34	Teachers Information
6.3.35	Universities List
6.3.36	VC / PVC History List
6.3.37	Guest Information List

Purpose of Screens

Screens 6.1 : Security Screen

Information in the Management Information System for University Administration is very important and confidential. Only authorised user should enter the MIS system. To avoid the un-authorised access to the MIS, password facility is provided.

If the entire password matches to the password defined in the system, then only access will be given.

Screen 6.2 : Main Menu

Management Information System for University administration is divided into FIVE parts i.e. General Administration, Examination, Finance and Account, Board of College and University Development and General Information. Through this menu, user can enter any one section to get the information. Depending upon the need of the user and permissions granted to the user, he can access the same part.

Screen 6.2.1.1 : Computers on the Campus

Various departments / sections in the university are having computers and other devices like printer etc. With use of this screen user can access the database on department code or department name combo box. After selecting a department / section all the related details of selected department like total computers available, make of computer, serial number, year of purchase, cost of unit, warranty period, Additional Accessories, printer make and specifications, its daily use, purpose and UPS details.

This screen also has the Add, modify and print option, with use of this option user can add new records or make changes in database. Through print option a hard copy will be printed on printer. Sample report is enclosed for reference.

Screen 6.2.1.2 : Designations in the University

As per the State / Central Govt. approval various posts are sanctioned to the university. With use of this screen, user can get the information regarding various designations with class, category and Pay Scale applicable to that designation.

With use of command buttons available in the screen, user can Add, Edit, Delete, View and Print the information from database.

With use of print option, a class wise, category wise list of designations with its pay scale will be printed on printer. Sample report is enclosed for reference.

Screen 6.2.1.3 and 6.2.1.3(A) : Information regarding various Departments

Each university is having various departments. With use of these screens, user can get detail information of each department like Head of Department, total teaching staff and total non-teaching staff, courses run at each department, number of students sex wise, Equipment in department with cost of each equipment. Library books and its cost, total class rooms, Built-up area, phone numbers, funding agency, conferences, seminars, workshops arranged by department in each year, total M.Phil, Ph.D. students etc.

All the above information is very useful to various sections. With use of command buttons user can Add, Modify, Delete or Print the information. Department screen is divided into two parts i.e. fixed information and year wise information. Sample report is enclosed for reference.

Screen 6.2.1.4 : Various Equipment's in University

With use of this screen user can get detail information of various equipments in various departments with its purpose, purchase date, cost, operator name, charges per hour, warranty period, department name etc. An user can get at a glance information of all types of equipments in very limited time.

With use of command buttons, user can Add, Modify, Delete and Print the equipment list. Even user can find total amount spent by university on various equipments. Sample report is enclosed for reference.

Screen 6.2.1.5 : Information Regarding Various Lecture Series

University arranges various lecture series on various occasions. Speakers from various places were invited to give their thoughts on the topic given. These lecture series are on various historical events or Important work done by famous persons in past years.

User can get information of all the lecture series held at university with other details like Year, lecture series name, Guest name, chairman, date and venue of the lecture.

With use of command button options user can Add, Modify, Delete or Print the list of lecture series. Sample report is enclosed for reference.

Screen 6.2.1.6 : Information Regarding University Library

University is having very big library. Many books, magazines, periodicals on various subjects are stored for reference. With use of this screen user can get information regarding total books, total periodicals, total journals, total computers and total cost of each of them. This information can be updated and through print option report can be generated. Sample report is enclosed for reference.

Screen 6.2.1.7 : Members Information

As per the Maharastra State University Act 1994

various bodies are formed like Academic Council, Senate and Management Council. Detail Information of each member like Name, Address, Phone Numbers, College code and period of membership can be available to the user. This information is useful to various sections, departments and also to the top management.

With use of Add, Modify, Delete and Print option, user can perform various operations on same data or he can print the list of members. Sample report is enclosed for reference.

Screen 6.2.1.8 : Phone Numbers Information

University is having its own PBX system for its campus wide sections / Departments. University also needs a easy access record of all other phone numbers like affiliated colleges, Govt. offices, VIP Guests, University officers etc.

With use of this screen, user can get the required phone number very easily. With use of command buttons, user can Add, Update, Delete and Print the telephone numbers list. With phone number user can also store a Room number and Building number. Sample report is enclosed for reference.

Screen 6.2.1.9 : Information Regarding Schemes

University receives various grants from various funding agencies. A State Government, Central Government, University Grants Commission etc are the bodies who sanction some amount every year for specific purpose within the university. University has to keep an account of such grants.

With use of this screen user can get information like Name of Department who received the grant, total amount sanctioned, actual amount received, actual amount spent, actual amount claim, scheme status, total teaching and

Non-Teaching posts sanctioned within the scheme and funding agency etc.

This screen gives very useful information to all levels of management in university to know the status of each scheme.

With use of command buttons user can Add, Modify, Delete or Print the schemes information. Sample report is enclosed for reference.

Screen 6.2.1.10 and 6.2.1.10(a) : Staff Information

University has many staff members. With use of this screen, user can get a detail information of each staff member like Name, Address, Phone number, qualification, Cast, Religion, Designation, Department, Date of Joining, Date of Retirement, Birth Date, Date of Increment, leave balance, bank account number, vehicle type and its registration number. In case of teaching staff how many conferences, workshop, seminars he has attended, any M.Phil, Ph.D. students, Research Paper Published and salary funding agency etc. are the main information which user can get. Various sections in the university also require this type of information very frequently like Establishment Section.

With use of command button functions user can Add, Modify, Delete and Print the information of staff. Sample report is enclosed for reference.

Screen 6.2.1.11 : Information of the Legal Section

University is having various legal matters in various courts. With use of this Screen, user can get the detail information of each case in court like case Number, Party Name, Cause, Court, Dates, Lawyer Name, lawyer address and phone number and decision if any - of any case. Many officers in the university require this information urgently.

With use of command button a user can Add, Modify, Delete and Print the information. Sample report is enclosed for reference.

Screen 6.2.1.12 : University Vehicles Information

University is having its own many vehicles. This screen is useful to keep record of each vehicle like Registration Number, type, year of manufacture, cost of vehicle, date of purchase, chassis number, engine number, fuel type, seating capacity, insurance company, insurance policy number, insurance date and insurance Expiry date etc. information will be available. This information will be useful to all levels of management in university.

With use of command button options, user can Add, Modify, Delete or Print the Vehicles information. Sample report is enclosed for reference.

Screen 6.2.2.1 : Faculty Information

University is having various courses under different faculties and each faculty has a Dean. With use of this screen a user can get information of each faculty with Dean of faculty and total number of colleges who are running the courses under same faculty.

With use of command button option user can Add, Modify, Delete or Print the faculty list. Sample report is enclosed for reference.

Screen 6.2.2.2 : Information of Various courses

University and its affiliated colleges runs various courses under various faculties. The courses may be from Ph.D, M.Phil, Master, Bachelor, Diploma, Certificate etc. With use of this screen, user can get detail information of each course with its faculty and type of degree.

With use of command button option user can Add, Modify, Delete and Print the course list. Sample report is enclosed for reference.

Screen 6.2.2.3 : Information of Various Examinations

University conducts various examinations in a year. With use of this screen, user can get detail information of each examination like name, faculty code, total colleges running same course, total Teaching staff, type of exam e.g. semester or Annual and parts of exam. This screen is useful to the students and their parents to know more information about the examinations.

With use of command button option user can Add, Modify, Delete and Print the information of examinations. Sample report is enclosed for reference.

Screen 6.2.2.4 : Information of Examination Centres

University conducts its various examinations at various examination centres. With use of this screen user can get detail information of each examination center like name of centre, is it available for March or October, seating capacity, total blocks available, total benches and total colleges under this centre etc. information is available through this screen.

With use of command button option Add, Modify, Delete or Print the list of examination centers. Sample report is enclosed for reference.

Screen 6.2.2.5 : Subject Wise Information

Each examination is having various subjects as per its syllabus. With use of this screen user can get information of each subject like examination name, subject code, subject name, maximum theory marks and minimum theory marks required for passing. Maximum practical marks and minimum practical marks for passing and maximum internal marks and minimum internal marks required for passing.

With use of command button option user can Add,

Modify, Delete or Print the subject wise information. Sample report is enclosed for reference

Screen 6.2.2.6 : Course Admission Information

University and its affiliated colleges run various courses. With use of this screen user can get detail information of each course like admission dates, exam code, name of the course, college code, last date of admission, last date with late fee, last date with super late fee, exam fee, late fee, super late fee to be paid by the student. It also shows the intake capacity of the course with reservation percentage for reserved category.

With use of command button option user can Add, Modify, Delete and Print the information of admission dates and for applicable to the course. Sample report is enclosed for reference.

Screen 6.2.2.7 : Student Information

Various students registered for various courses in University or in affiliated colleges. With use of this screen an user can get detail information of each student like his permanent registration number, name, permanent address, temporary address, course name, year of admission, college code, phone number etc. This information is very useful to various sections in the university.

With use of command button options user can Add, Modify, Delete and Print the student information. Sample report is enclosed for reference.

Screen 6.2.2.8 : Examination Schedules information

University conducts various examinations twice in a year. With use of this screen user can get detail information of each exam schedule like exam name, starting date, last paper date, year and month of exam and morning or evening session.

This screen is also useful to students who can know the dates of examination commencement and end. With use command button option, user can Add, Modify, Delete and Print the information of exam schedule. Sample report is enclosed for reference.

Screen 6.2.2.9 : Examiners Information

University appoints various teachers from the colleges as an examiner to examine the answer sheets, for paper setting and for conducting practical examinations etc. With use of this screen user can get detail information of each examiner like name, subject, address, phone number, post graduate teaching experience, under graduate teaching experience, qualification and college code.

With use of command button options user can Add, Modify, Delete and Print the examiner list. Sample report is enclosed for reference.

Screen 6.2.2.10 : Result Information

Results of the examinations conducted by the university are required to be declared with in stipulated time, usually university has to declare the result of any examination on or before the 30th day after the last paper or maximum of 45th days as per the University Act – 1994.

With use of this screen, user can get information of result like exam code, total registered students, total absent students, class obtained, seat number, last date for revaluation and verification of answer books, total first class, second class and pass class students with percentage of passing.

With use of command button option user can print the result on printer. This screen is useful to the students also. The output report prints the result in a format of graph, which is easy to understand. Sample report is enclosed for reference.

Screen 6.2.2.11 : Prizes Information

After conducting the yearly examination and result declaration university authorities declare the prizes for various courses and subjects to the meritorious students. With use of the this screen user can get detail information of prizes like year and month exam, name of the prize, prize amount, nature of prize, PRN, marks obtained, marks out off, class obtained, seat no. etc.

With use of print option user can print the list of Prizes on printer. Sample report is enclosed for reference.

Screen 6.2.2.12 : Convocation Information

To award the degrees, every year university organizes a convocation function. All the students who have completed the course, will be awarded a Degree Certificate.

User can get detail information of all previous convocations held like year, faculty code, total degrees, total In-person and In-absentia, total boys and girls and total Ph.D students., Hon. Chief Guest of function, Hon. Vice Chancellor and Hon. Pro-Vice Chancellors name, etc.

With use of print option user can print the convocation report, same report also have a graphical representation for better understanding. Sample report is enclosed for reference.

Screen 6.2.2.13 : Central Assessment Center Information

For evaluation of answer sheets, university authorities setups an Central Assessment Center at various places. One Director is appointed to manage the center.

With the use of this screen, user can get the information like Center code, Center Name, Month and year of Exam, Director name, Examinations name, total examiners appointed, total moderators appointed and total non teaching staff appointed.

With use of command button options user can Add, Modify, Delete and Print the list. Sample report is enclosed for reference.

Screen 6.2.3.1 : Annual Maintenance Contract Information

The various equipments like computers, printers etc purchased by university are to be properly maintained. Therefore university enters into an Annual Maintenance contract with various companies. With use of this screen user can get detail information of each equipments maintenance contract like sr no of equipment, AMC from to date, AMC amount, name of AMC company, address, phone number, pager number, fax number etc.

With use of command button options user can Add, Modify, Delete and Print the list of AMC equipment. Sample report is enclosed for reference.

Screen 6.2.3.2 : University Budget Information

University has to prepare a financial Budget every year to plan its income and expenditure on various activities in a year. Finance Committee will sanction every department /section a sum amount and within that limit they have to plan their activities. Every time while any purchase request from department/section, budget provision has to be verified and then only permission for expenditure will be allowed by Budget Section.

With use of this screen user can easily get the information of each budget head like department name, actual budget, actual estimate, revise estimate, budget year, budget head, balance amount.

With use of command button option user can Add, Modify, Delete and Print budget information. Sample report is enclosed for reference.

Screen 6.2.3.3 : Payment Information

With use of this screen user can get the information of payment made to each employee in a particular month on various heads like salary, advance, over time, leave travel concession, leave surrender etc. other information like bank account number, date of deposit, employee name, etc information will be available.

With use of command button option user can print the list of employees for a given month with their payment.

Payment report is also available department wise, so that user can get the information of expenditure on a particular department also. Sample report is enclosed for reference.

Screen 6.2.3.4 : Bank Deposits Information

With use of this screen, user can get the detail information of various deposits made by university in various banks. Other information like Bank Name, type of deposit, Amount deposited, period of deposit, rate of interest, date of deposit, date of maturity and maturity amount.

This screen is useful to Accounts Section and Top management people to plan their resources.

With use of command button option user can Add, Modify, Delete and Print bank deposit information. Sample report is enclosed for reference.

Screen 6.2.3.5 : Income Tax Information

With use of this screen, user can get the detail information of Income Tax paid by the university, other information like year of tax paid, department name, type, chalan number, return submitted on, return claimed amount etc.

With use of this screen user get total tax paid and tax return pending with income tax department. With use of Add, Modify, Delete and print option user can modify the information. Sample report is enclosed for reference.

Screen 6.2.3.6 : Rate Contract Information

To purchase the frequently required items by various departments/sections, university enters into an Rate Contract with the suppliers to provide various items as when required for an agreed amount for a specific period.

With use of this screen user can get detail information of all the items for which rate contract is made e.g. Item name, item cost, contract from, contract up to, party name, party address, party phone number, mobile number and pager number.

With use of command button options, user can Add, Modify, Delete or print the information. Sample report is enclosed for reference.

Screen 6.2.4.1 : Affiliated Colleges Information

University has various affiliated colleges. With use of this screen user can get detailed information of each affiliated college like college name, year of establishment, management name, address, principal name, qualification, college phone number, fax number, type of affiliations, total teaching staff, total non-teaching staff, names of the courses run, total girls and boys students, area of colleges, total built-up area, total seating capacity, exam centre for March or October etc.

With use of command button option user can Add, Modify, Delete and Print the college information. This screen is very useful to all sections of university for their day-to-day working. Various reports can be generated from this information. Sample report is enclosed for reference.

Screen 6.2.5.2 : University Organization Charts

As per the University Act 1994, there are in all four major parts / divisions at university. viz. General

Administration, Examination, Finance and Accounts Section and Board of College and University Development. Each division has various sections. With use of this screen user can get detail information of each division from top to bottom level management.

Screen 6.2.5.4 : University Information

With use of this screen user can get the information of various universities like name of the Vice-Chancellor and Pro-Vice Chancellor, University Area, year of establishment, total affiliated colleges, address, phone numbers, fax and E-mail address.

With use of command button option user can Add, Modify, Delete and Print university information. This information is very useful to various sections in university for day-to-day administration. Various reports can be generated from this data. Sample report is enclosed for reference.

Screen 6.2.5.5 : Hon. VC / Hon. PVC History

With use of this screen user can get detail information of all the previous Hon. Vice Chancellors and Hon. Pro-Vice Chancellor of the University with their period of service, qualification, previous institution etc.

With use of command button option user can Add, Modify, Delete and Print the information on printer. Sample report is enclosed for reference.

Screen 6.2.4.2 : Information regarding Research work at University

Research is major activity of any university. Various research students make research in various subjects under the guidance of subject expert.

With use of this screen user can get detail information of Faculty Name, Subject Name, Area of Research, Name and address of research student, Name and address of his/her guide, Registration date etc.

This information is useful to office administration and also to outside student who needs information regarding his related subject and various topics, which are already selected by various students for research.

This screen also has add, modify and print option, with use of this option user can add new records or make changes in database. Through print option a hard copy can be printed on printer. Sample report is enclosed for reference.

Screen 6.2.4.3 : Information regarding college and University Teachers

Common database is created for all the teachers in all the affiliated colleges and in University departments. User can get detail information of teachers like Name, qualification, Special Subjects, total teaching Experience at Graduate level and at post graduate level, Joining date, date of Retirement etc.

This information is also useful for Appointment Section to appoint examiners for paper setting and conducting practical examinations and answer sheet evaluation. With use of Command button option, user can add new records or make changes in database. Through print option a hard copy can be printed on printer. Sample report is enclosed for reference.

Screen 6.2.5.6 : Information regarding University Guests

University arranges various seminars, lecture series, functions like convocation etc. various guests were invited to attain the same.

With use of this screen user can get detail information of all university guests like Guest Name, institution, address, phone number etc.

With use of this data, letters can be send to all guests or Address ship can be printed and same can be paste on envelope.

This screen also has add, modify and print option, with use of this option user can add new records of make changes in database. Through print option a hard copy can be printed on printer. Sample report is enclosed for reference.

Screen 6.2.5.1 : Universities Information Screen

With the use of this screen user can get the fixed information related to the university like year of establishment, total affiliated colleges, total students, courses conducted, total Teaching and Non-teaching staff, university area, built-up area etc.

With use of this screen user can get all such information at a glance.

Screen 6.2.5.3 : Awards Information Screen

Every year sportsmen of the university participate in various games. With use of this screen user can get the detail information of various awards won by the university at the various games.

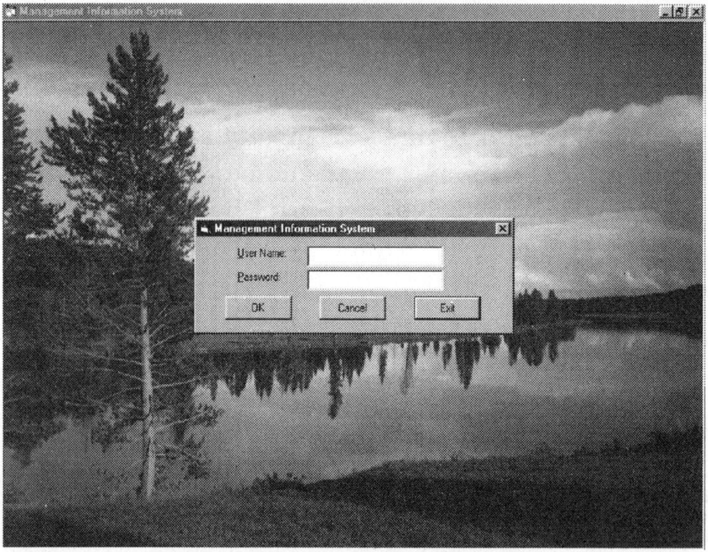

Screen 6.1 : Security Screen

Command Button Functions :-

Ok : After entering the password click ok button.

Cancel : To quit without entering password.

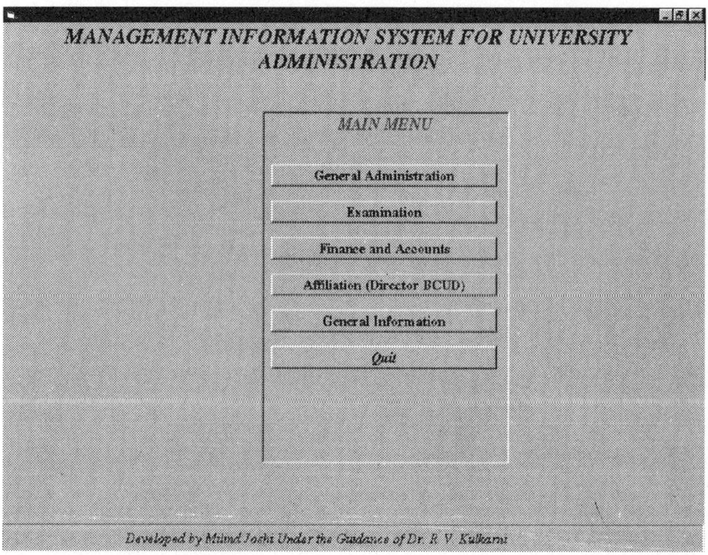

Screen No. 6.2 : Main Menu Screen

Command Button Functions

General Administration : To get sub menu of General Administration.

Examination : To get sub menu of Examination.

Finance & Accounts : To get sub menu of Finance & Accounts.

Affiliation (Director BCUD) : To get sub menu of Affiliation.

General Information : To get sub menu of General Information.

Quit : To quit the Main Menu.

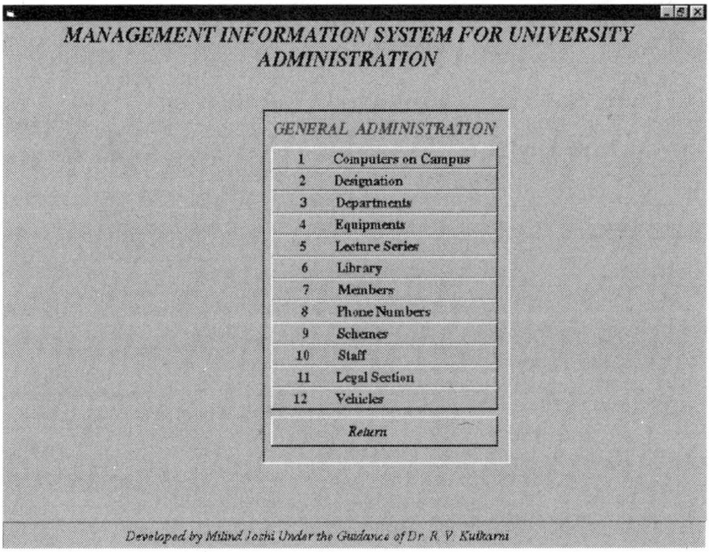

Screen 6.2.1 : General Administration Information Screen

Command Button Functions

Return : Return to Main Menu.

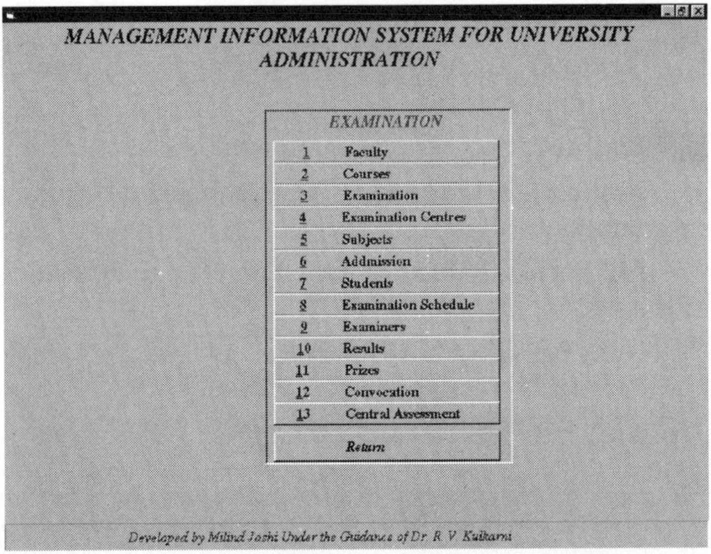

Screen 6.2.2 : Examination Information Screen

Command Button Functions :-

Return : Return to Main Menu.

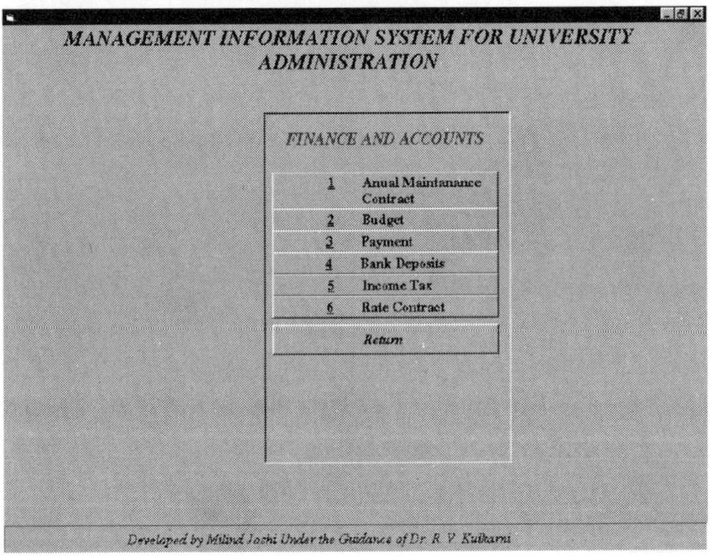

Screen 6.2.3 : Finance & Accounts Information Screen

Command Button Functions

Return :- Return to Main Menu.

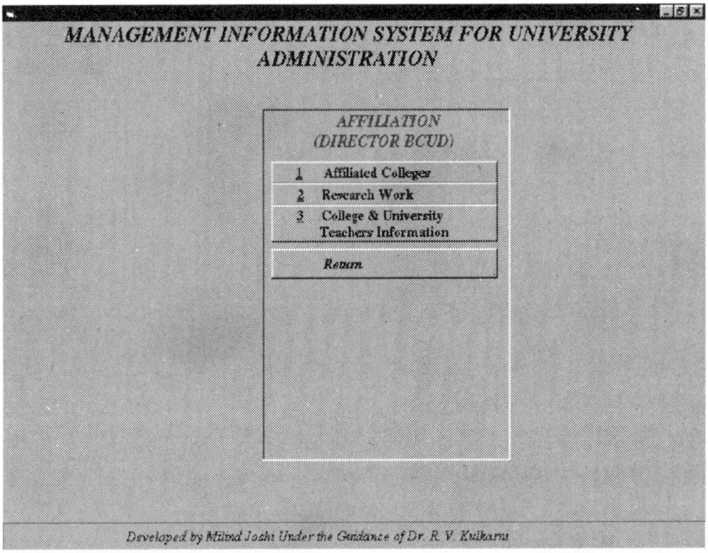

Screen 6.2.4 : Affiliation Information Screen

Command Button Functions

Return :- Return to Main Menu.

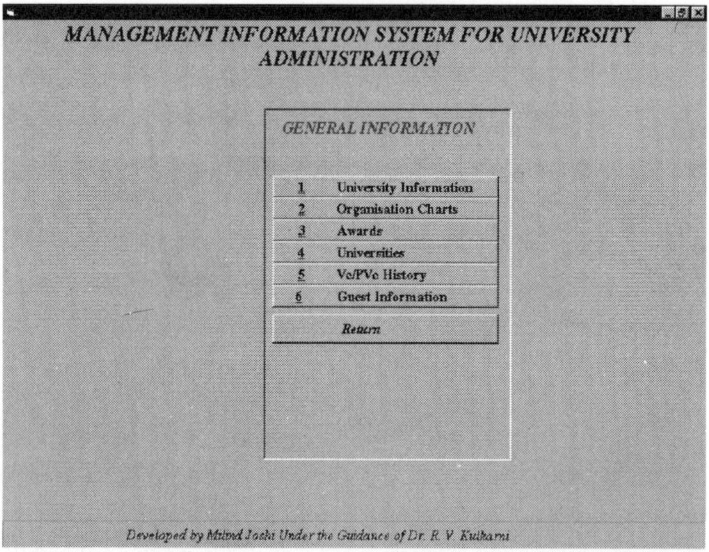

Screen No. 6.2.5 : General Information Screen

Command Button Functions

Return : Return to Main Menu.

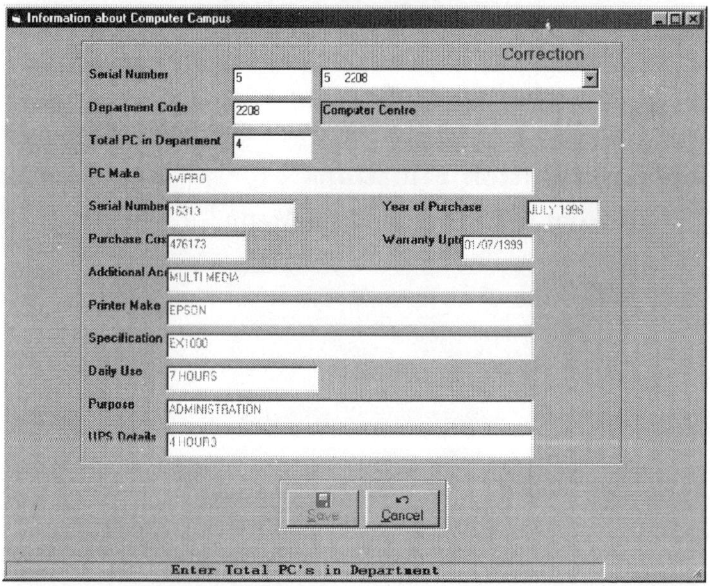

Screen 6.2.1.1 : Computers on Campus Information Screen

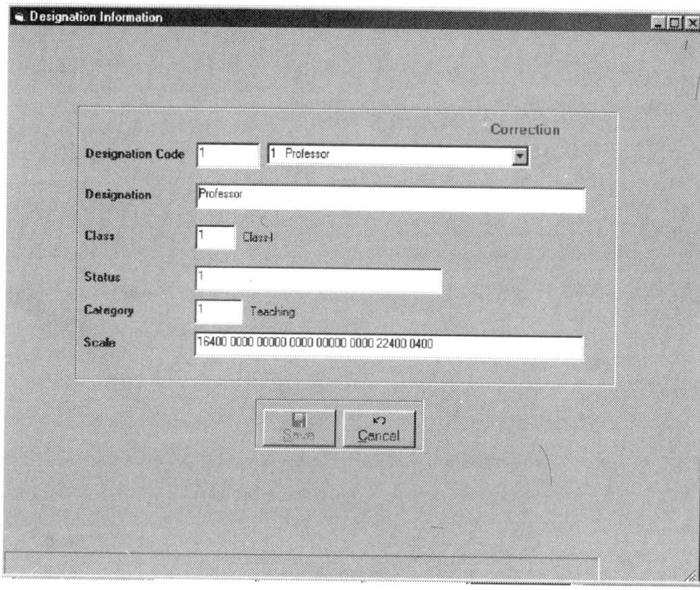

Screen 6.2.1.2 : Designations Information Screen

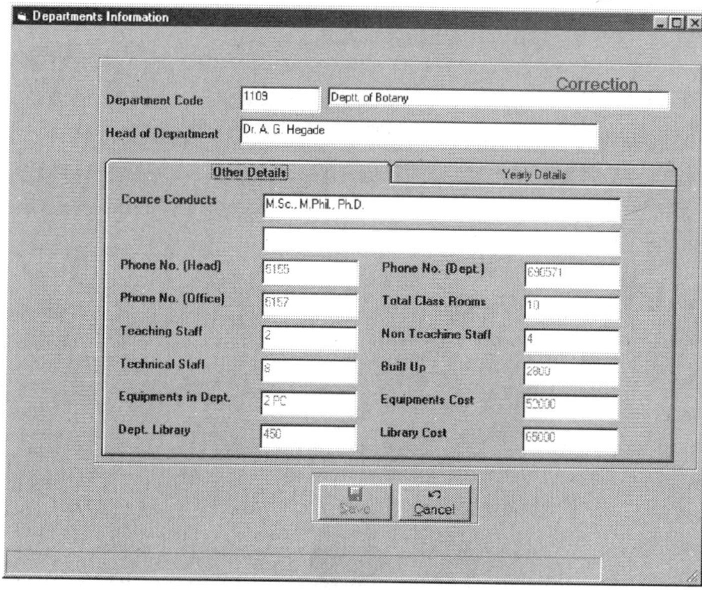

Screen 6.2.1.3 : Departments Information Screen

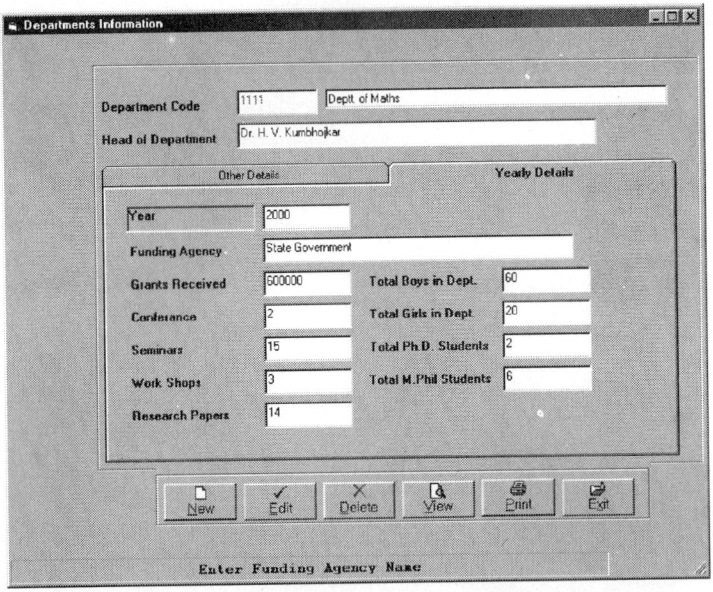

Screen 6.2.1.3(a) : Departments Information Screen

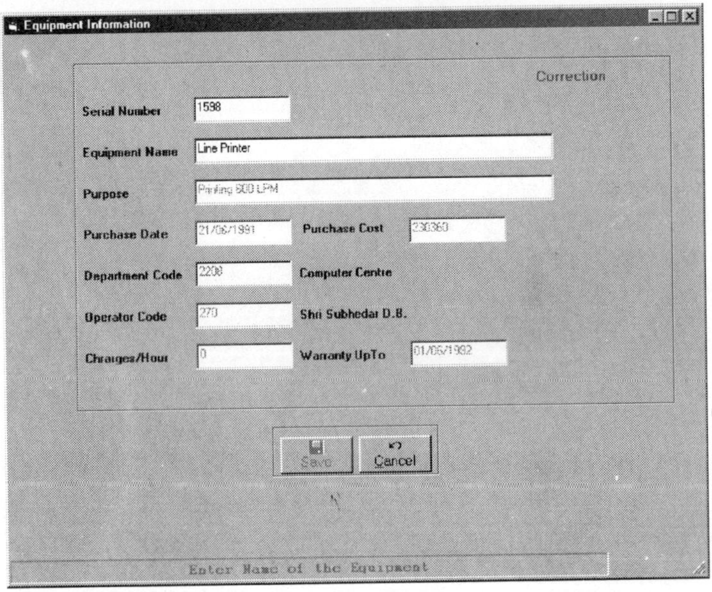

Screen 6.2.1.4 : Equipments Information Screen

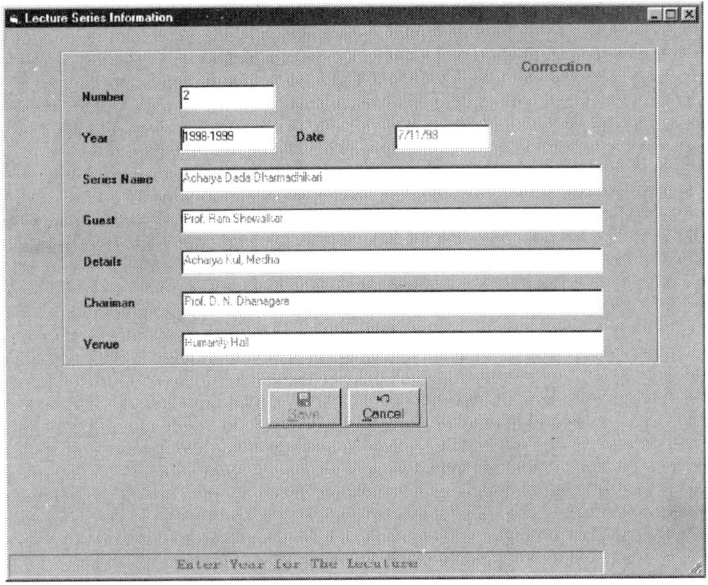

Screen 6.2.1.5 : Lecture Series Information Screen

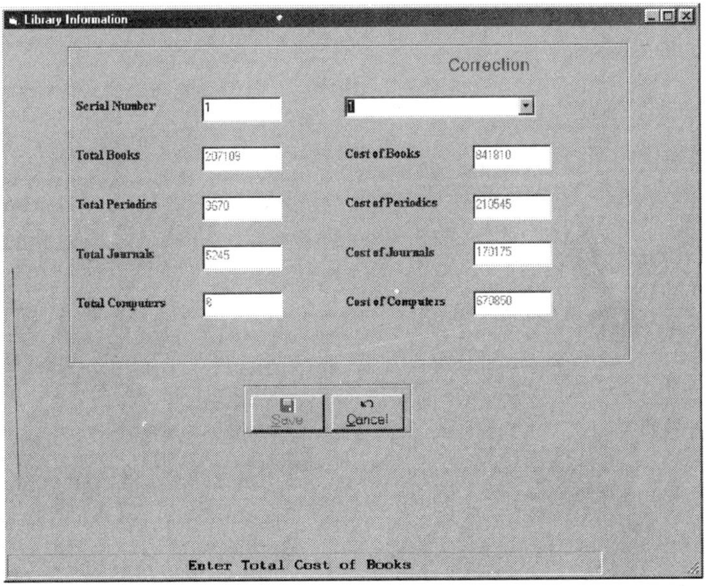

Screen 6.2.1.6 : Library Information Screen

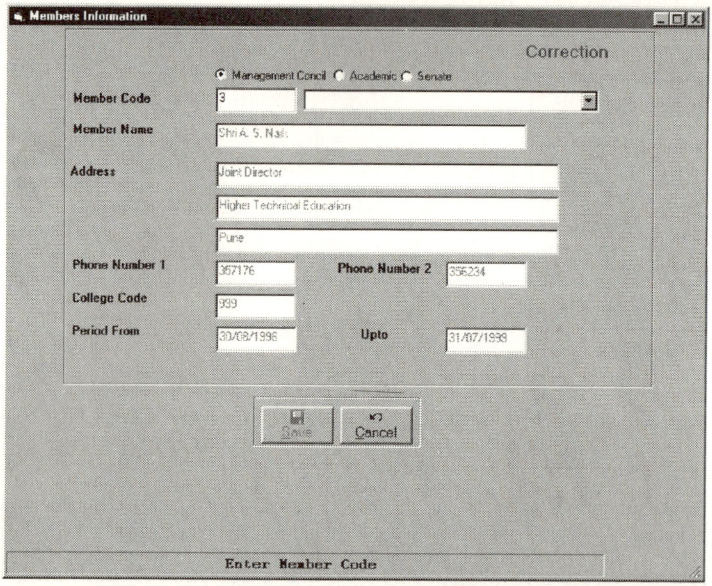

Screen 6.2.1.7 : Members Information Screen

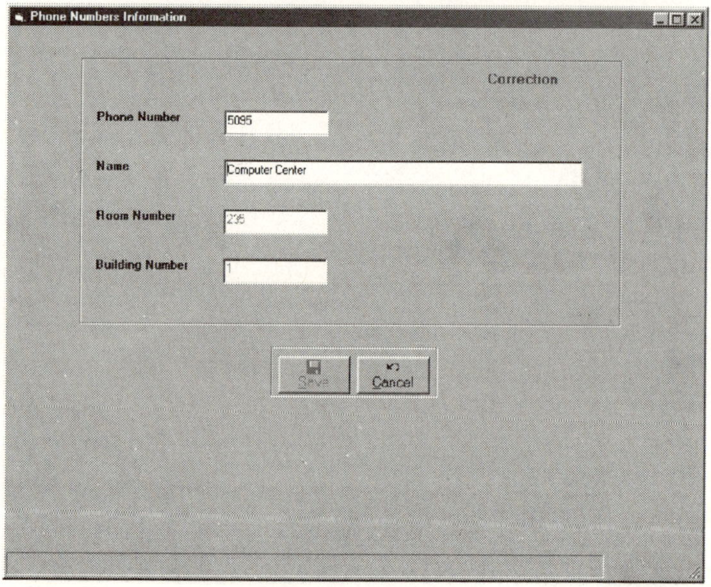

Screen 6.2.1.8 : Phone Numbers Information Screen

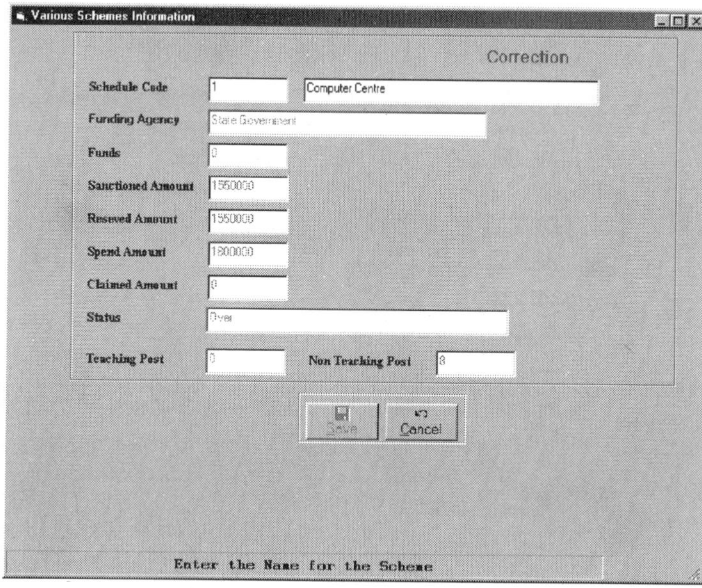

Screen 6.2.1.9 : Various Schemes Information Screen

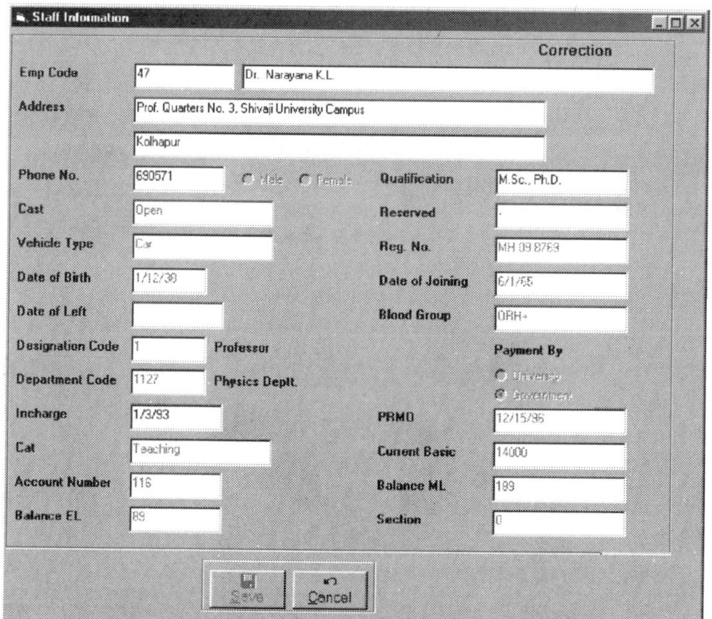

Screen 6.2.1.10 : University Staff Information Screen

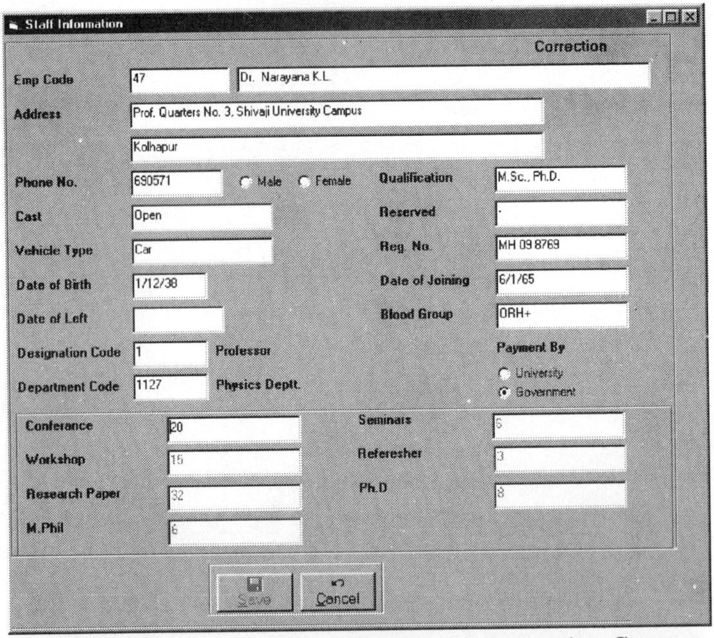

Screen 6.2.1.10 (a) : University Staff Information Screen

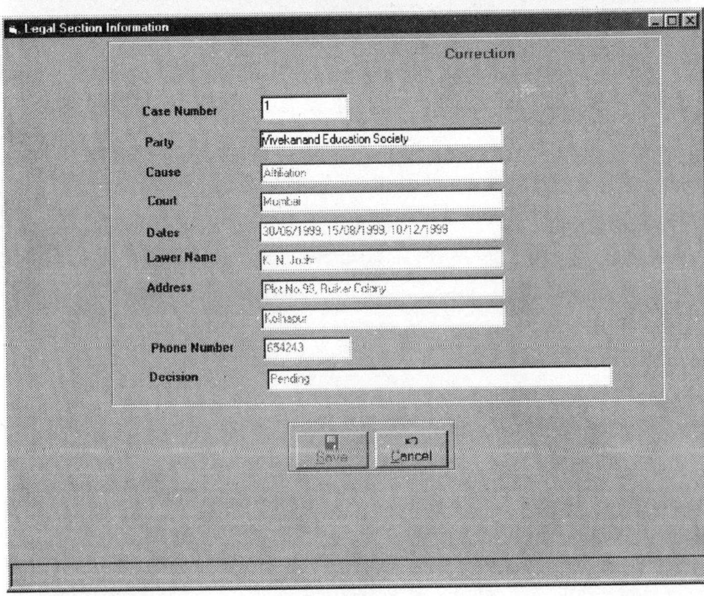

Screen 6.2.1.11 : Legal Section Information Screen

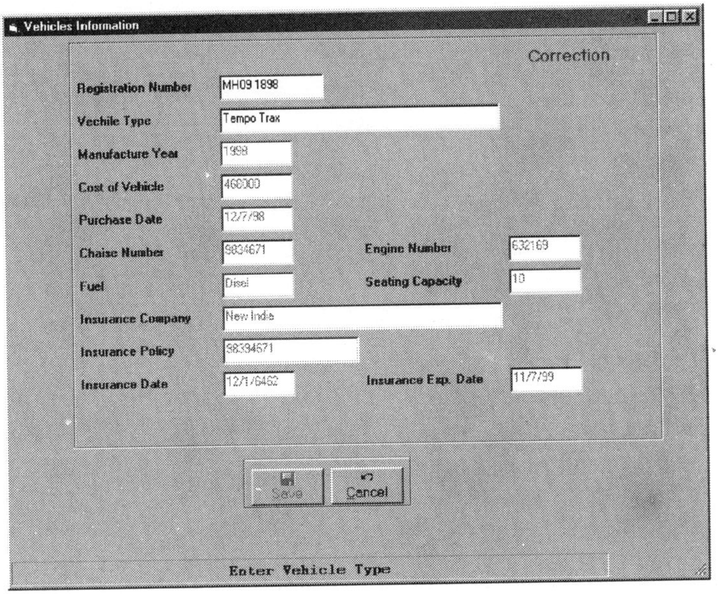

Screen 6.2.1.12 : University Vehicles Information Screen

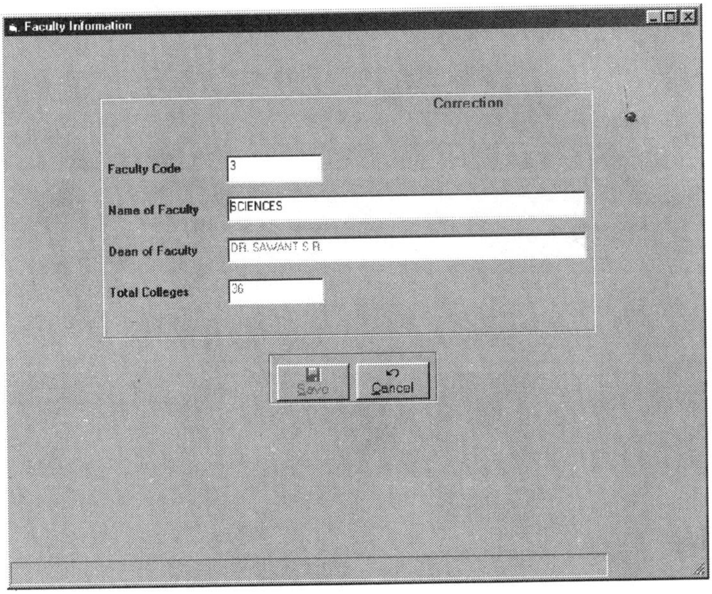

Screen 6.2.2.1 : Faculty Information Screen

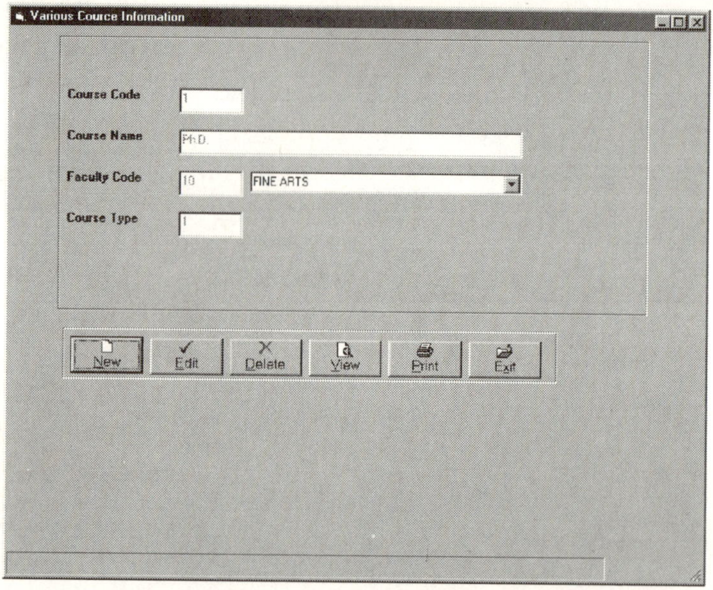

Screen 6.2.2.2 : Various Courses Information Screen

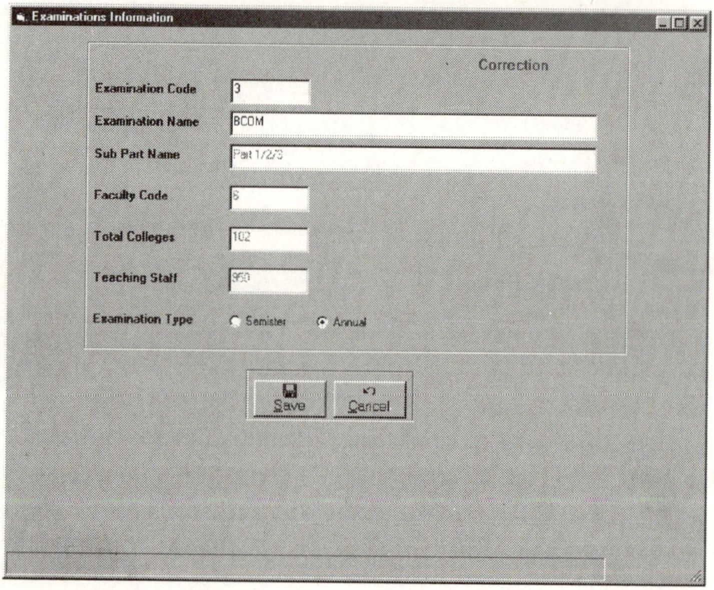

Screen 6.2.2.3 : Various Examination Information Screen

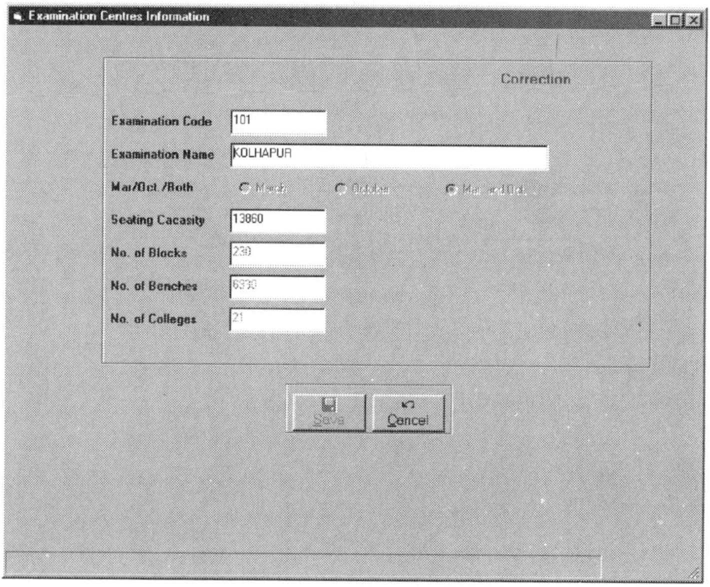

Screen 6.2.2.4 : Examination Centres Information Screen

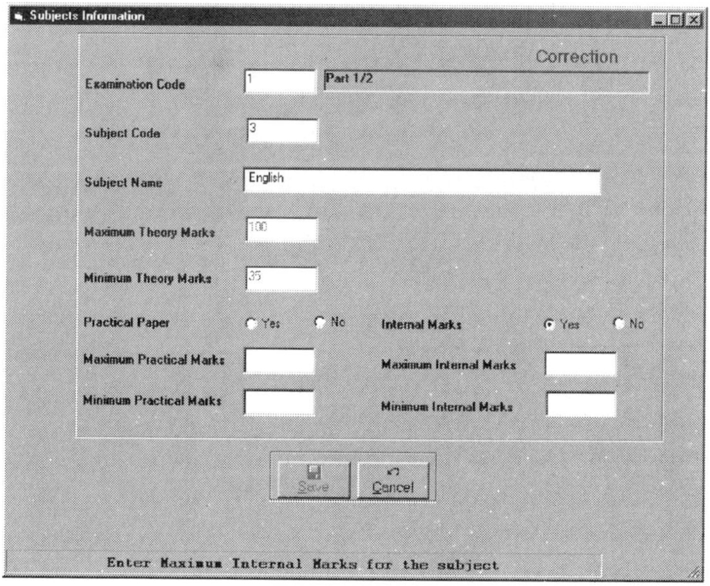

Screen 6.2.2.5 : Various Subjects Information Screen

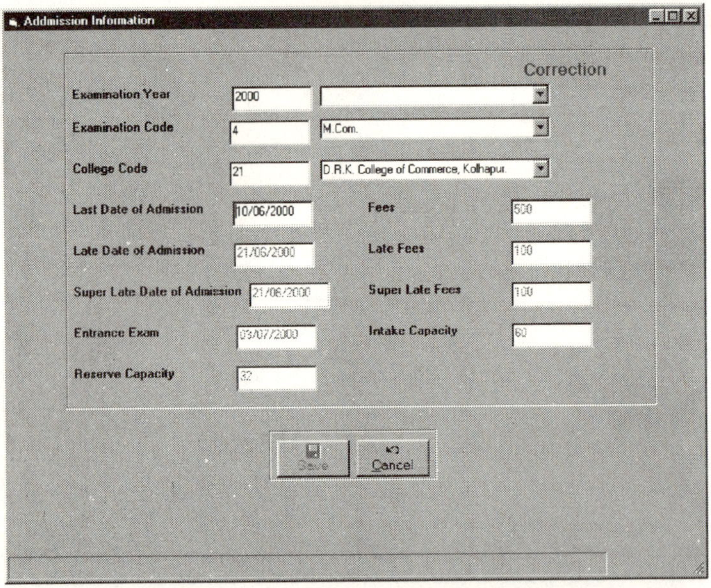

Screen 6.2.2.6 : Admission Information Screen

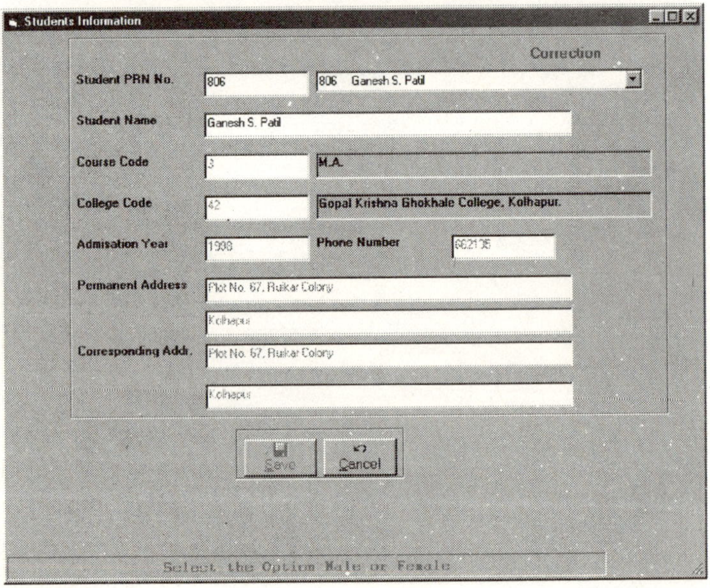

Screen 6.2.2.7 : Students Information Screen

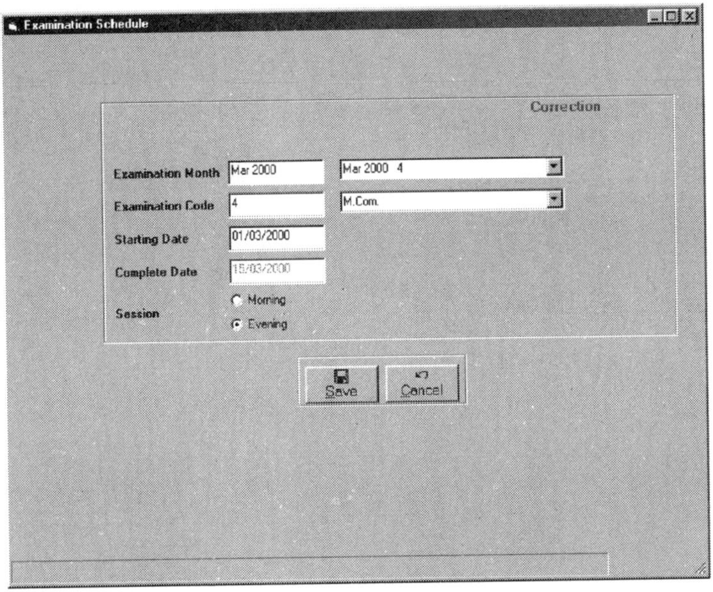

Screen 6.2.2.8 : Examination Schedule Information Screen

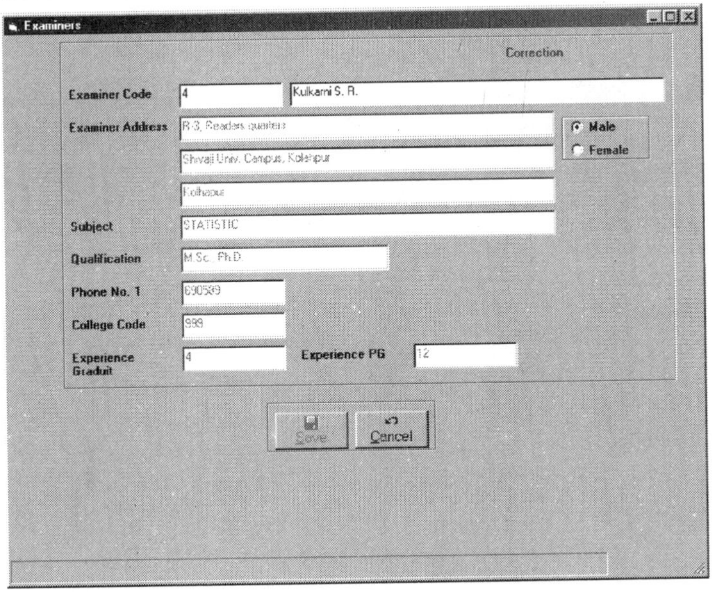

Screen 6.2.2.9 : Examiners Information Screen

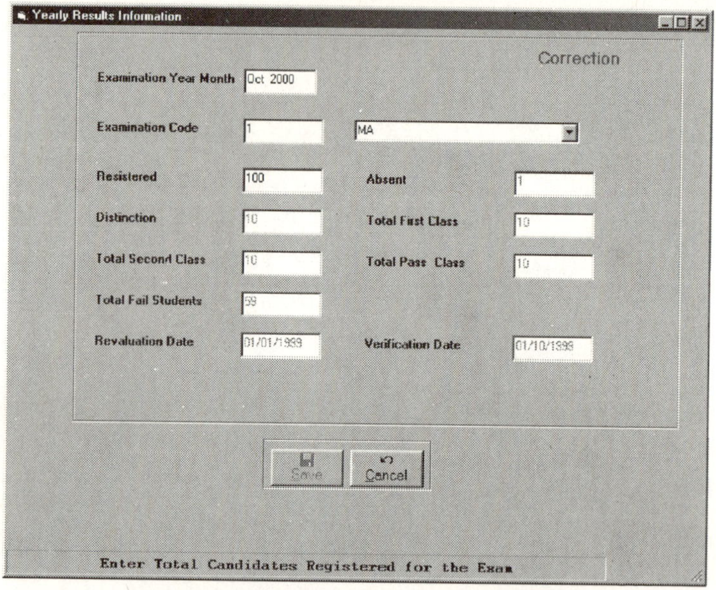

Screen 6.2.2.10 : Yearly Results Information Screen

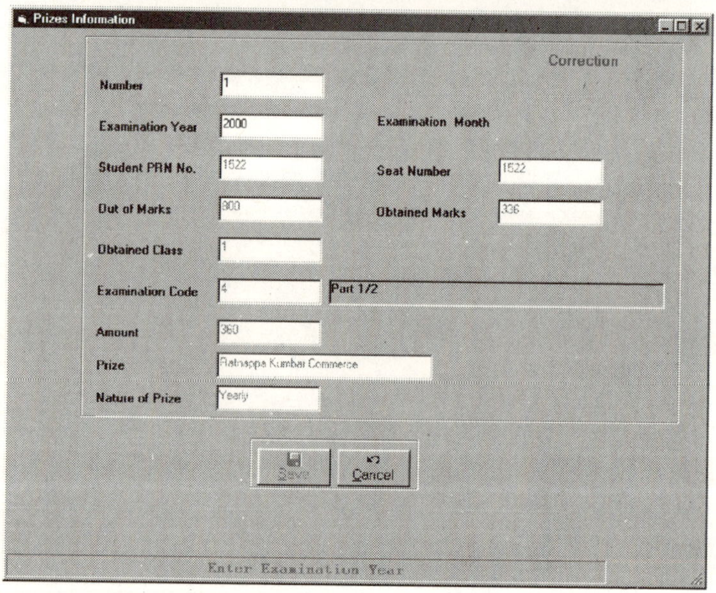

Screen 6.2.2.11 : Prizes Information Screen

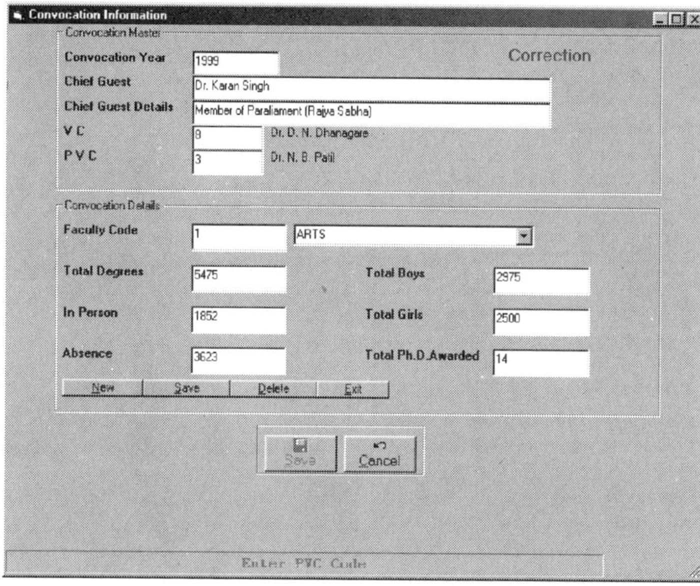

Screen 6.2.2.12 : Convocation Information Screen

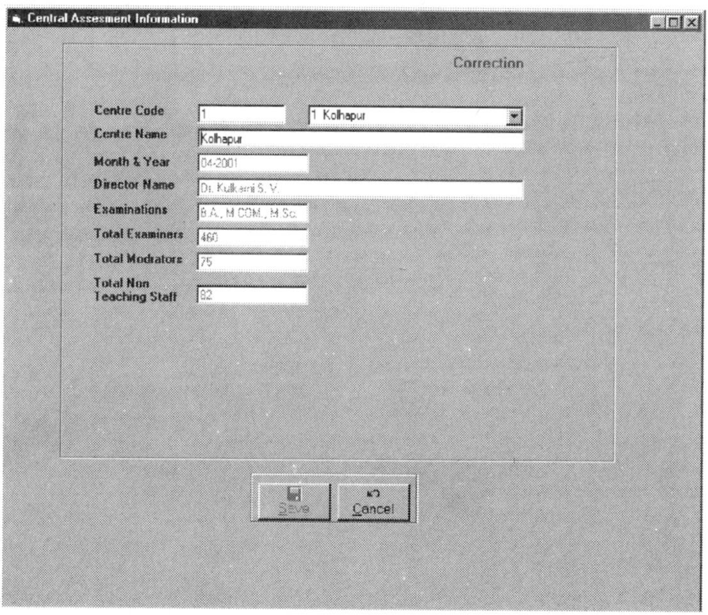

Screen 6.2.2.13 : Central Assessment Information Screen

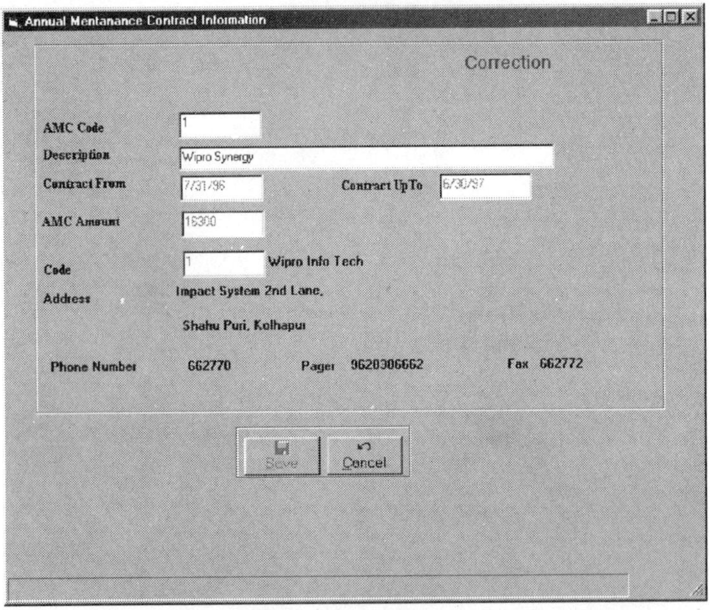

Screen 6.2.3.1 : Annual Maintenance Contract Information Screen

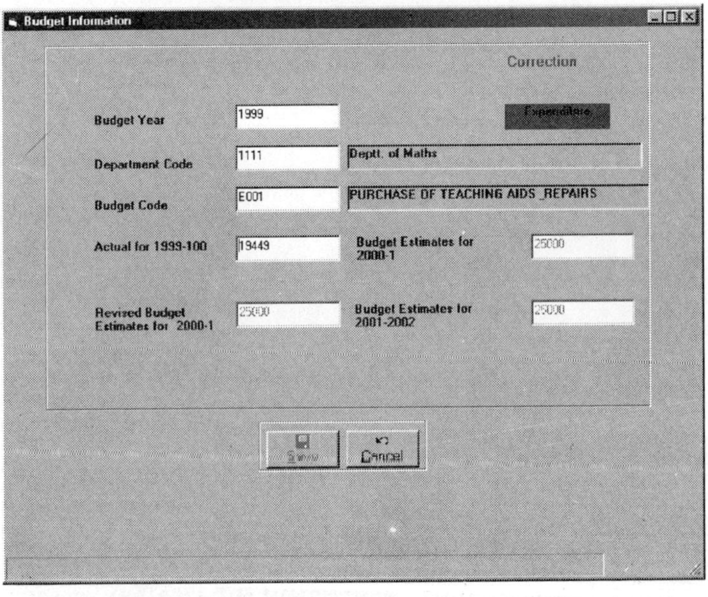

Screen 6.2.3.2 : Budget Information Screen

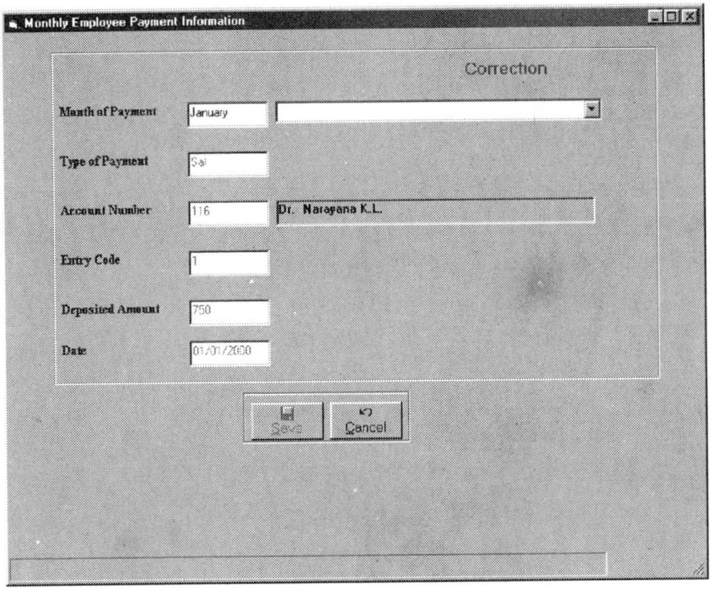

Screen 6.2.3.3 : Payment Information Screen

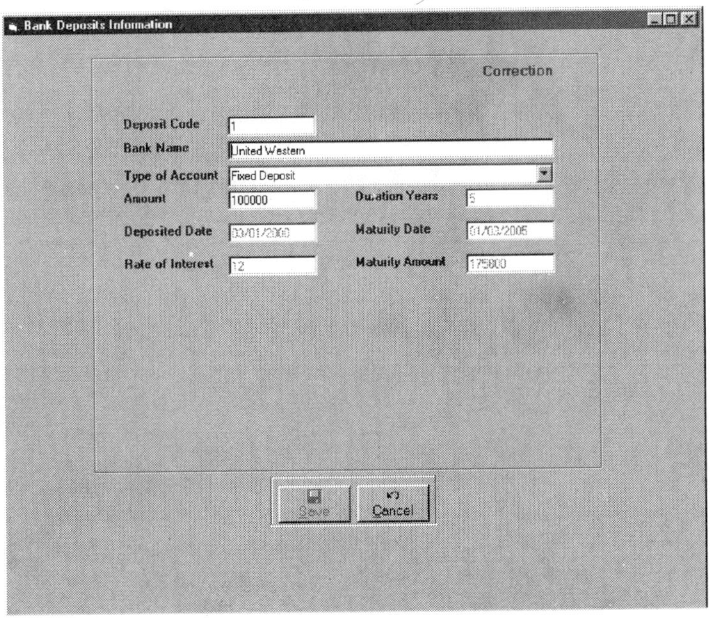

Screen 6.2.3.4 : Bank Deposits Information Screen

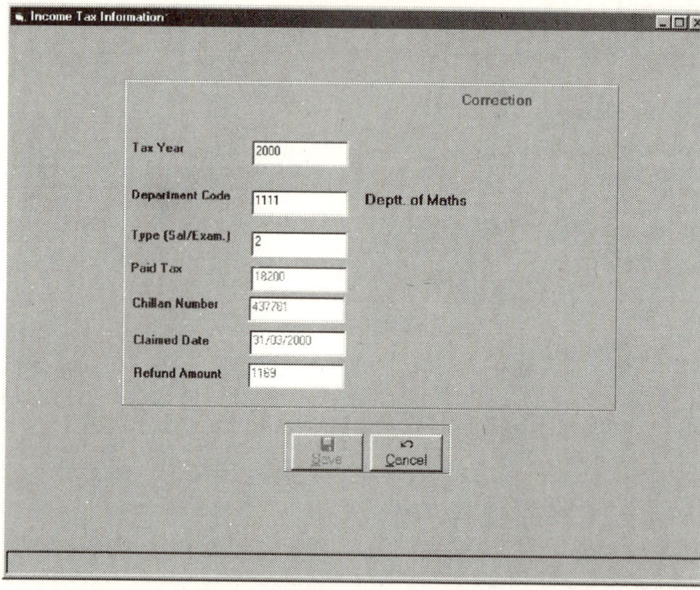

Screen 6.2.3.5 : Income Tax Information Screen

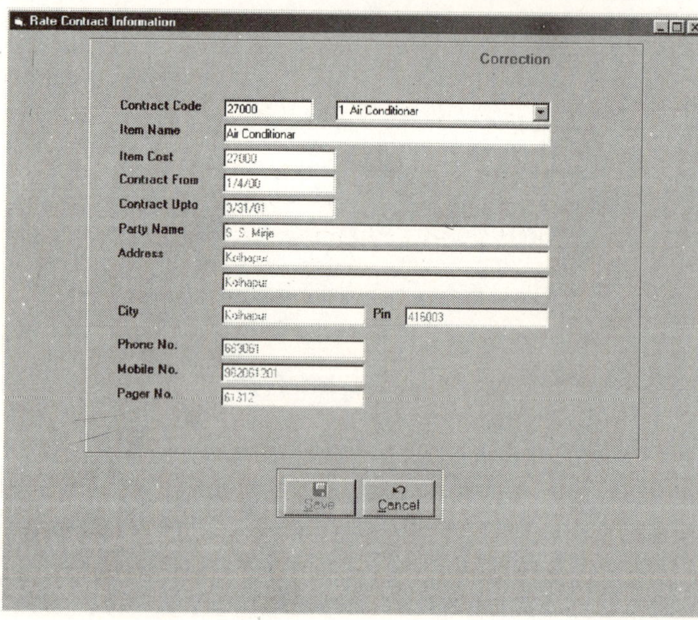

Screen 6.2.3.6 : Rate Contract Information Screen

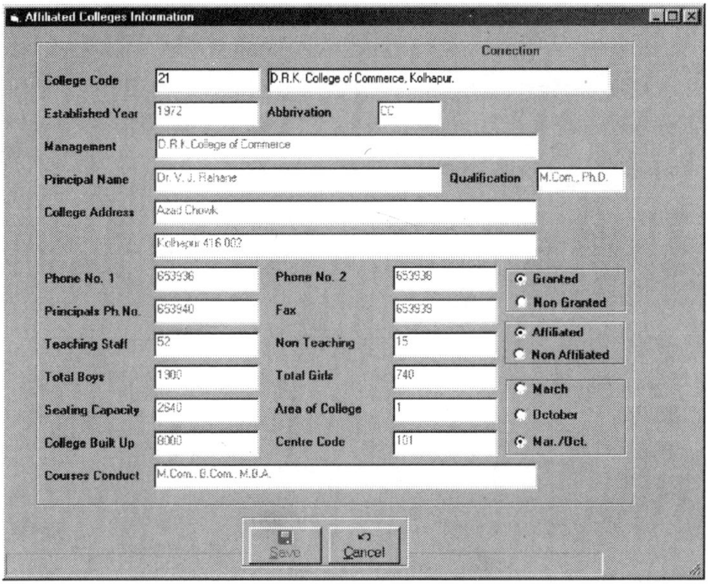

Screen 6.2.4.1 : Affiliated Colleges Information Screen

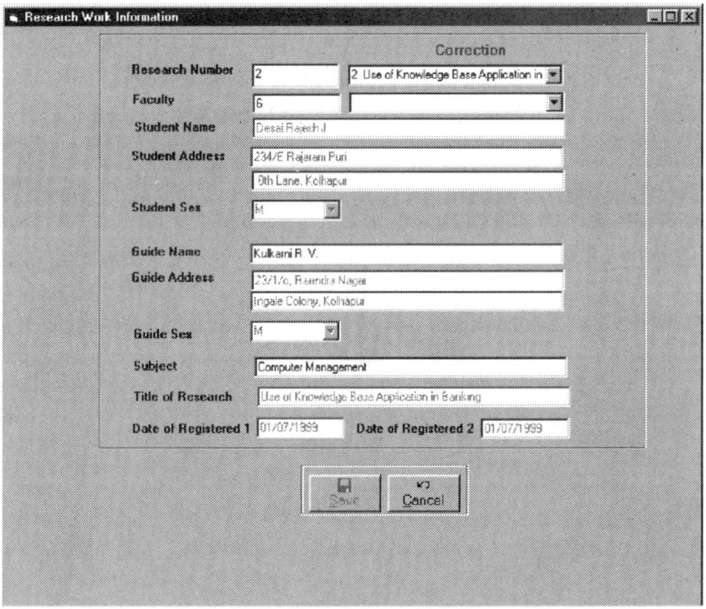

Screen 6.2.4.2 : Research Work Information Screen

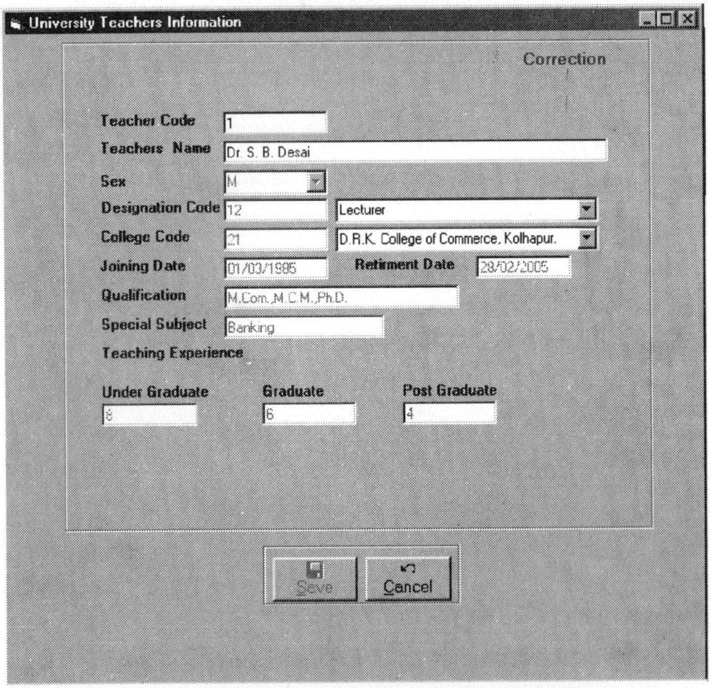

Screen 6.2.4.3 : College & University Teachers Information Screen

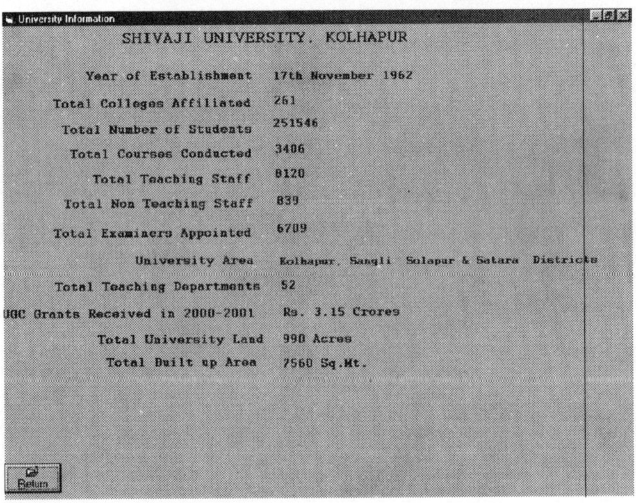

Screen 6.2.5.1 : Universities Information Screen

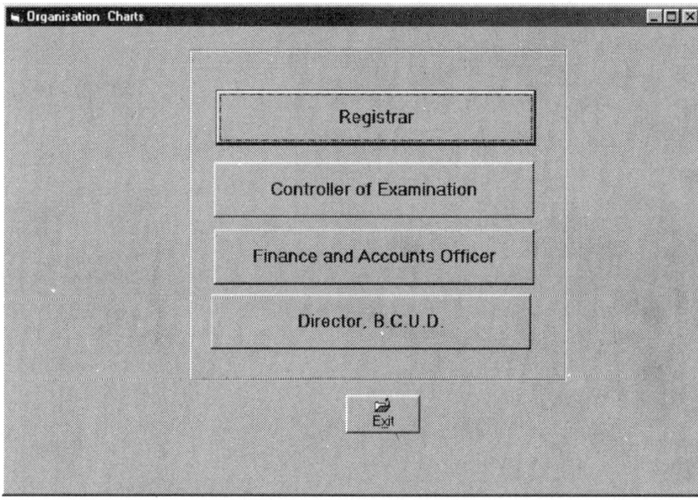

Screen 6.2.5.2 : University Organization Chart Information Screen

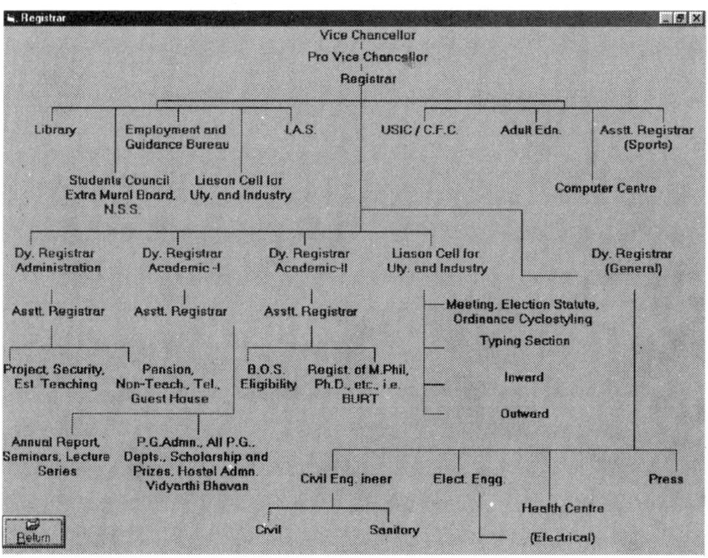

Screen 6.2.5.2 (a) : General Administration Information Screen

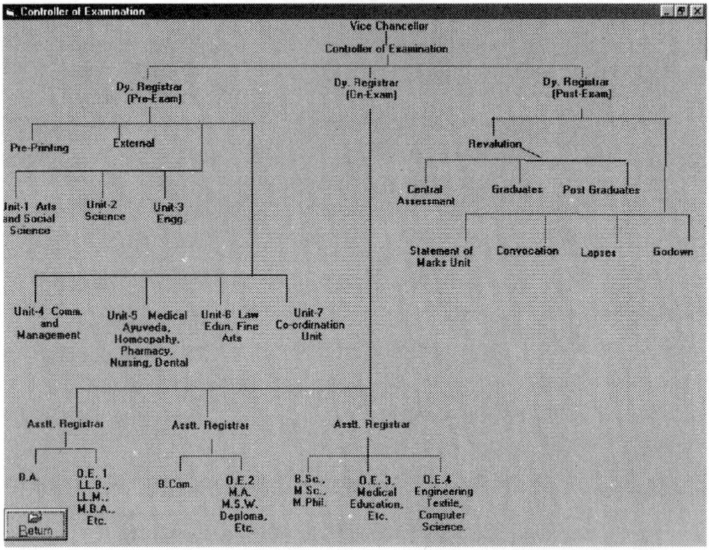

Screen 6.2.5.2 (b) : Controller of Examination Information Screen

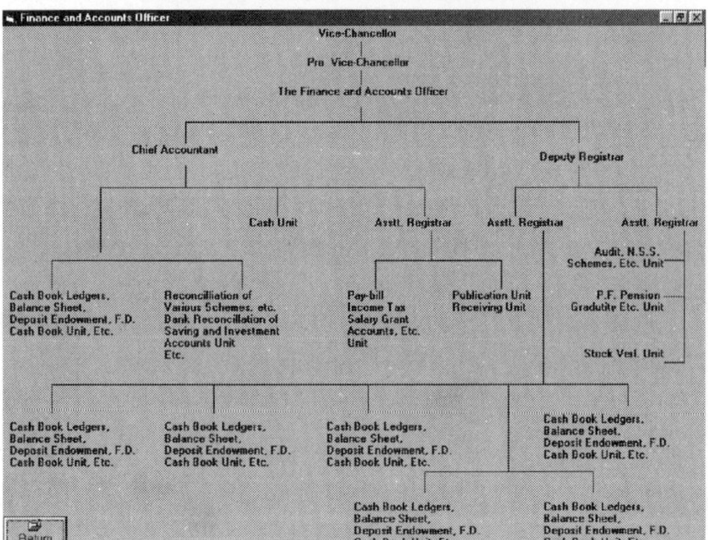

Screen 6.2.5.2 (c) : Finance & Accounts Officer Information Screen

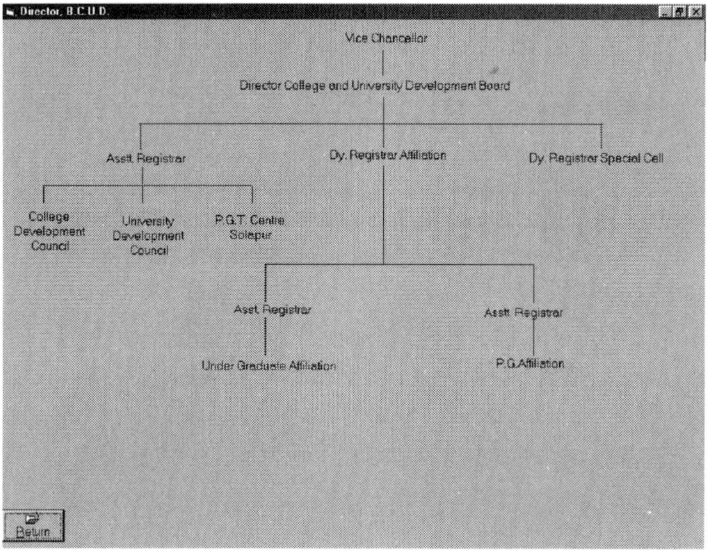

Screen 6.2.5.2 (d) : Director B. C. U. D. Information Screen

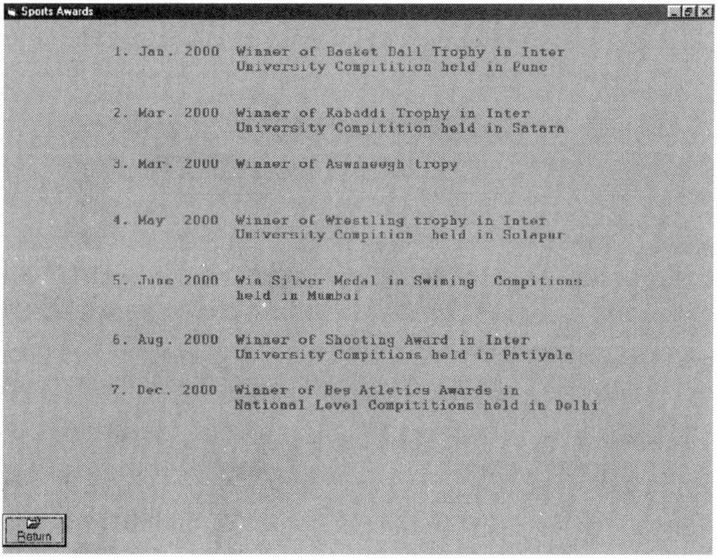

Screen 6.2.5.3 : Awards Information Screen

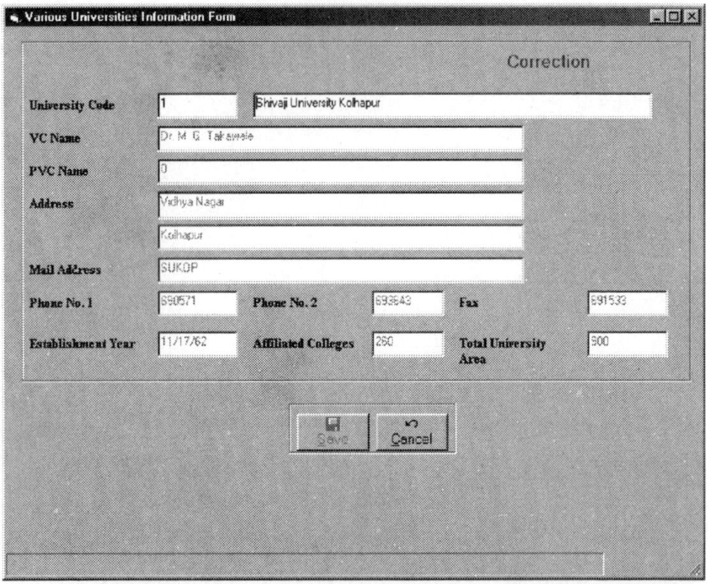

Screen 6.2.5.4 : Universities Information Screen

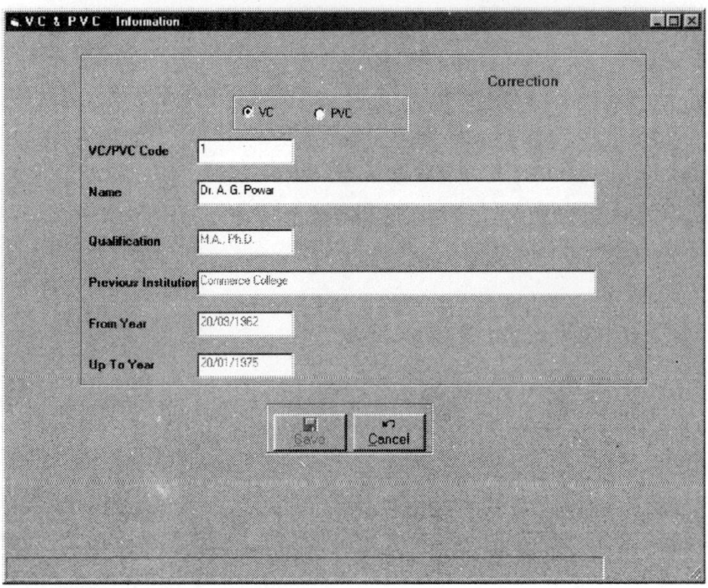

Screen 6.2.5.5 : VC & PVC Information Screen

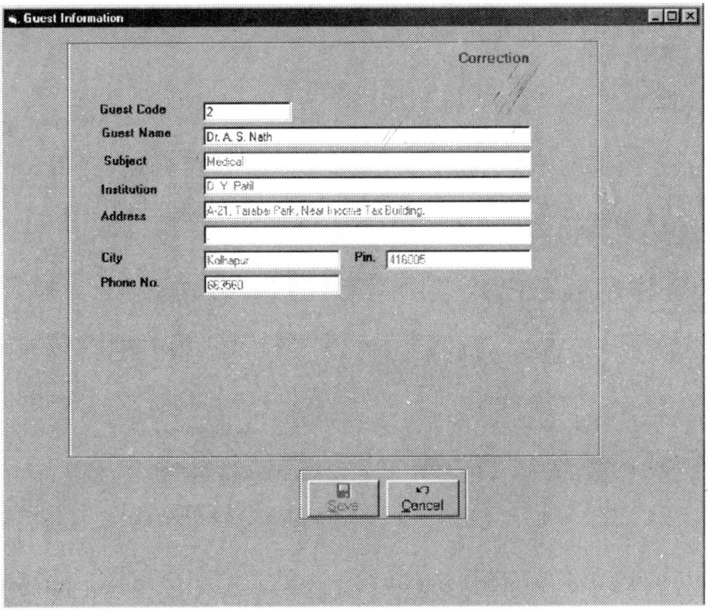

Screen 6.2.5.6 : Guest Information Screen

7
Implementation and Cost Benefit Analysis

ABSTRACT

In this chapter the researcher has made cost benefit analysis after implementation of functional model of MIS in two sections of the university. Total cost of manual work and computerised work are compared with live data.

7.1. INTRODUCTION

Researcher has implemented a functional model of MIS in two sections of the University namely Convocation and Budget Section. Required reports are generated using MIS for both sections. Working of each section with current man power are discussed below -

1. Convocation Section

Once in a year university organize a convocation function to award the degrees to successful students. The students who had passed various courses are required to apply in prescribed forms to the university. Convocation section processes all these forms and performs following operations on the forms –

* Checking the forms
* Sorting the forms as per course, class obtained and on alpha
* Verifying the result with office copy of the related course ledger
* Preparing the name list of students
* Preparing the summary report
* Printing the degree certificate
* Dispatch the convocation program with name list number to all students
* Distribution of degree certificates and modification of degree certificates in case of any mistakes

Present Staff at Convocation Section

Sr. No.	*Post*	*Nos.*	*Salary Monthly*	*Total*	*YearlySalary*
1.	Superintendent	1	10,000	10,000	1,20,000
2.	Asst. Supdt.	1	8,000	8,000	96,000
3.	Sr. Clerk	2	7,000	14,000	1,68,000
4.	Jr. Clerk	4	6,000	24,000	2,88,000
5.	Daily Wages (for 3 months)	6	2,000	12,000	36,000
	Total				**7,08,000**

If Computer is used :

Sr. No.	*Items*	*Nos.*	*Cost*	*Total*
1.	Cost of Hardware	5 Nodes	50,000	2,50,000
2.	Operators	2	8,000	1,92,000
3.	Cables and Other Exp.	—	—	50,000
4.	Printer	1	25,000	25,000
5.	Other costs	—	—	50,000
	Total			**5,67,000**

Total costing of Manual Work Rs. 7,08,000

Total costing if MIS is used Rs. 5,67,000

It is observed from the above figure that university spends yearly an amount of Rs. 7,08,000 per year on salary only. If computers are installed there will not be any maintenance cost for three years (Most of the MNC branded computers provide at least three years comprehensive warranty) and by considering other costs the University has to spend Rs. 5,67,000 per year.

2. Budget Section

Budget section controls all the financial provisions of the university. University authorities assign fix amount to each budget head of various departments/sections. It also decides various income and expenditure budget heads and depending upon income from various source expenditures are allowed to minimize the deficit. Before any sanction to expenditure, each folder has to route through budget section after checking budget provision and actual balance remaining. Budget section performs following duties :-

* Preparation of Budget
* Allotment of Receipt and Payment bill
* Updating on ledger as per the receipt.
* Budget curtailment (if any)
* Remarks on folders of various departments/sections

Present Staff at Budget Section

Sr. No.	*Post*	*Nos.*	*Salary Monthly*	*Total*	*Yearly Salary*
1.	Supritendent	1	10,000	10,000	1,20,000
2.	Asst. Supdt.	1	8,000	8,000	96,000
3.	Sr. Clerk	2	7,000	14,000	1,68,000
4.	Jr. Clerk	3	6,000	18,000	2,16,000
	Total				**6,00,000**

If Computer is used :-

Sr. No.	*Items*	*Nos.*	*Cost*	*Total*
1.	Cost of Hardware	5 Nodes	50,000	2,50,000
2.	Operators	2	8,000	1,92,000
3.	Cables and Other Exp.	—	—	50,000
4.	Printer	1	25,000	25,000
5.	Other costs	—	—	50,000
	Total			**5,67,000**

Total costing of Manual working Rs. 6,00,000

Total costing if MIS is used Rs. 5,67,000

Note : One main MIS server with hubs and switches will be kept at Main Building. All nodes will be connected to this server.

From the above costing it is clear that due to use of MIS, we can save the considerable amount of money. Two trained operators will train existing staff of the concern section and slowly they will start working independently on computers. In short computer staff will train one-by-one to all the administrative staff to use computers for their day-to-day working.

The initial feed back collected by the researcher while implementation from the user had been positive. The university officers have certainly stated that this system can be employed to expedite decision process and thereby save time and other costs.

8
Suggested Network, Hardware and Software Requirements for MIS in University Campus

ABSTRACT

In this chapter the researcher has given a detailed network solution for campus wide network of university. He has studied the Present Internet Network and Present Hardware at university and then new network solution is designed. With a combination of fiber and copper cable's network is designed so that it will be optimally used with minimum cost. At the end total approximate cost of network is given by considering the present Hardware and Software costs.

8.1. INTRODUCTION

Researcher has developed a functional model of MIS for University Administration. To have an optimal use of information technology, every university must go for campus wide Networking or Intranet. With use of Internet, all section / departments will be connected to each other via computers which will help in faster communication between sections. It is also one step ahead to 'Paper Less Office' technique.

8.2. Network Suggested

Various departments of the university are located all over the campus of the university. In the suggested network basically there are three groups of network and within these groups various nearby departments are connected (as shown in Figure No. 8.1).

Network 1 : Chemistry Dept., Zoology Dept., Botany Dept., Physics

Dept., Maths Dept., Stats Dept., CFC Unit, Environmental Science Dept. and Bhasha Bhavan.

Network 2 : Main Building and Library Building.

Network 3 : Geography Dept., Education Dept., Shahu Research Center and Humanities Building.

All the three networks are connected with Fiber cable (as shown in Figure No. 8.2 and Figure No. 8.3). As observed Network –1 has more load than other two networks, Layer 3 switch is used for Network –1 and Layer –2 switch is used for both Network – 2 and Network –3 (as shown in Figure No. 8.3).

The proposed MIS server will be kept in Main Building (Second Floor) which is having 100 Mbps switch and will be uplink from Library Switch (as shown in Figure No. 8.4).

The suggested network also has the facility of Internet access. University has taken a leased line from telephone department. Figure No. 7.5 shows the detail connections from modem, router, server and switches.

University Main Building i.e. Administration of University is managed from this building. All the sections like General Administration, Finance, Affiliation and

Examination are located in this building. Offices of the Hon. Vice Chancellor, Hon. Pro-Vice Chancellor, Registrar, Controller of Examinations and Finance and Accounts Officer are also located in this building. In the suggested network, all the rooms in the Main Building are given nodes (as shown in Figure No. 8.6, Figure No. 8.7 and Figure No. 8.8).

Figure No. 8.10 shows how the Departments/ Sections are connected via Cat-V UTP cable, 24 Ports Jack Panel, Ethernet Switch and Information outlets.

Figure No. 8.11, 8.12 and 8.13 shows technical details of Layer-2 switch and Layer-3 switch.

Before going for campus wide network we must study, what type of cables to be used and are they really suitable for proposed network in long run.

Cabling : Several years ago when UTP copper cabling was thought to have reached its peak with category 5 at 100 MHz, many users and vendors alike turned their attention to optical fiber as the natural migratory path for IT infrastructure. It offered solutions to all the shortcomings of UTP, it had higher bandwidth, greater allowable distances, increased security, complete immunity from RFI and EMI, closer allowable proximity to power cabling, and it posed no threat to peoples health from radiation.

Despite this intrinsic superiority of optical fiber over copper, today we still find copper cable and connector manufacturers fervently trying to extract every last bit-per-second out of it. But, instead of investing all this energy into copper, why don't we just install optical fiber every where ? It boils down to one major factor : COST.

What's happening today

Most network cabling being installed today is UTP, compliant to the draft "Enhanced Category 5" or "Cat 5t" standards issued by EIA / TIA and ISO respectively. These performance criteria cater for the ultra high speed network applications that are currently on the drawing board such as Gigabit Ethernet, and 1.2 GBps + ATM Systems, that are designed to take information at these speed to the desk. That's about 100 to 1000 times faster than what most users are experiencing on the common shared 10 Base T Ethernet System.

The lengths of cabling required in most offices these days are well within the 100 meter distance limitation of copper, so it will accommodate the physical dimensions of the office also. Essentially, optical fiber offers advantages in every aspect over UTP, but these advantages are not critical to the day-to-day issues of an office network and consequently, the cost differential becomes hard to justify for most organistions.

Cost Comparisons

Taking a typical office floor of 100 work stations, let's compare the cost of installing a single 4 pair UTP channel with a single multi-mode fiber channel. The UTP channel will be rated to enhanced category 5compliance, comprising of cabling, panels, workstation out lets, and patch leads at both ends of the channel, The fiber channel will comprise of FDDI rated multi-mode cable, patch panels, workstation out lets and patch leads at both ends.

It is quite apparent take OFTD does not come near the cost of UTP. In fact it is over three times the cost, and that's just for the passive part of the network. That cost differential is further increased if we add the cost of active equipment, namely hubs and network Interface Cards(NIC's).

The above cost comparison demonstrates the primary reason why UTP continues to be the medium of choice in the horizontal channel to the workstation.

Therefore, Researcher has suggested a combination of UTP and fiber cable network for the university. As shown in the detailed charts enclosed.

Network Distribution Schemetic

* Internet (I-NET) Department located at USIC building is the location for Mail / Internet Server and super stack of switches.

  Proposed MIS Server will be locate at computer centre, main building. Connections to MIS server will be established using existing fiber network as shown in diagram.
* Single mode and multi mode fiber cables running to various departments. Within departments all PC's connected over copper link (UTP category 3 a cable)
* To achieve high bandwidth and better speed, the switch used at I-net is layer 3 switch and all other are layer 2 switches.
* The links between two various departments shown here are actually termination points of fiber. The fiber link having terminated at one department moves forward to other department.
* This schematic shows fiber terminating and Interfacing device, which is called LIU (Light Interfacing Unit)
* All necessary fiber cores are terminated in this box and using special molded cable, it is connected to Active device like switches or router.
* The diagram depicted here shows Inter – departmental fiber connectivity.
* This diagram shows a typical local network structured cabling scenario.
* The components shown here are 100 Mbps switch which is inputted to the fiber link from I-Net, which

is then inserted to Jack Panel, the number of ports on the panel could be more than or equal to the number of PC's to be connected.

* This diagram shows how MIS server is going to be accessed.

  The MIS server is on the same Internet Network Via a Layer – 2 100 Mbps switch, and the fiber link from switch at library is given to this switch and the copper link goes out to all PC's in various departments / sections.

* This schematic shows two sub-networks, one comprises library and main building network and other Humanity and other nearby networks within campus and those outside the campus.

* This diagram shows location of main building (Ground, First and Second Floor) from where MIS server is going to be accessed.

* This is how MIS server is linked with existing Internet Network and is made accessible to those who are authorised to access the server.

* Location of MIS server in main building is at Room No 325, Computer Centre.

* This is the schematic of how the MIS server is interfaced and made accessible to various sections / departments.

* The availability of server thought whole network is achieved by connecting the server to main stack at I-Net.

Technical Details of components used in suggested Network :

1. Layer 2 Switch

Layer 2 is a repackaging of multi-port bridging technology that provides significant performance improvements and increased scalability. With layer-2 switching, frames are switched based on MAC address information.

2. Layer 3 Switch

Layer 3 integrates routing functions into a switch, providing LAN routing at near switching speeds, and that can help to improve network performance significantly. With layer-3 switching frames are switched based network layer information

3. LIU

Life Interface Unit (LIU) where we are connecting the fiber backbone using ST connector and ST coupler.

4. Patch Cords

A flexible piece of cable terminated at both ends with connectors. Used for interconnecting circuits on a patch panel or cross connect.

5. Router

Routers separate broadcast Domains and are used to connect different networks. Routers use Layer switching to route a packet.

6. Modem

A Modem is a device that lets your computer communicate with other computers over a standard telephone line. It is short for **mo**dulator/**dem**odulator. This term means that the modem converts the digital information from your computer to an analog signal that can travel over phone lines. Then the receiving modem converts the analog signal back to a digital signal for the receiving computer to work with.

7. TX Port

TX support a 100 mb/s transmission rate over two pairs twisted pair cabling. It uses one pair of wires for transmitting data, and the other pair for receiving data. The two pairs of wires are bundled into a single cable that may often include two additional pairs of wires. If present, the two additional pairs of wires must remain unused since 100 Base-TX is not designed to tolerate the "cross talk" that can occur when the cable is shared with other signal. Each of the cable is terminated with an 8 position RJ-45 connector, or "jack".

8. FX Port

FX supports a 100 Mb/s transmission rate over two fiber optic cables. It allows maximum segment lengths of 412 meters for half-duplex links, and 2000 meters or more for full-duplex links.

List of Hardware/Software Required for Proposed Campus Network

University can implement the MIS system by installing a higher end server having disk mirroring and duplex features at the central location of university. All nodes should be connected to this server through fiber optics (as shown in network diagram) cable. The proposed system calls for following Hardware and software.

1. Hardware

Sr. No.	*Description*	*Qty.*	*Cost*
PART - A- SERVERS AND NODES			
A1	**Primary Internet + MIS Server – Compaq ProLiant ML330** / Coppermine PIII 866MHz/133MHz FSB/ 256KB On-chip Cache/64MB SDRAM + ADDITIONAL 64 MB RAM/ 4 memory banks total/ 5x1" Non-HotPlug Drive Support/ 6 slots & 5 Bays/9.1GB Wide Ultra2 SCSI 3 Non Pluggable disk drive.	2	2,11,000.00
A2	**Secondary Internet Server**-Compaq Deskpro SB/ Coppermine PIII 866MHz/		

Sr. No.	*Description*	*Qty.*	*Cost*
	133MHz FSB/ 256KB On-chip Cache/ 64MB SDRAM/20GB Ultra ATA HDD/ 15" Compaq Color Monitor/ Keyboard/ Mouse	1	55,000.00
A3	Additional 18 GB SCSI HDD for MIS Server	1	30,000.00
A4	**NODES** Compaq Deskpro SB/ Coppermine PIII 866MHz/133MHz FSB/ 256KB On-chip Cache/64MB SDRAM/20GB Ultra ATA HDD/15" Compaq Color Monitor/ Keyboard/ Mouse	50	27,50,000.00
PART - B- LEASED LINE COMPONANTS			
B1	CISCO Router	1	1,05,500.00
B2	Leased Line Modem Pair	1	81,250.00
B3	CAB V.35 MT Cable	1	7,000.00
PART - C – NETWORKING COMPONANTS			
C1	Layer 3 Stackable Switch	1	4,46,250.00
C2	16-port 10/100 Stackable Switches	2	1,50,000.00
C3	16-port 10/100 Non-Stackable Switches	10	4,00,000.00
C4	12 Core outdoor armoured cable – sm	NA	6,60,000.00
C5	6 Core outdoor armoured cable – sm	NA	5,00,000.00
C6	CAT 5, 4 Pair, UTP Cable, 15000 ft.	NA	93,750.00
C7	Other Passive Components	NA	3,00,000.00
PART - D – IMPLEMENTATION AND CONFIGURATION			
D1	**Leased Line Termination & Cabling** : 1. End to End termination. 2. Network Design. 3. Switch/Hub Configuration. 4. Security Implementation.	NA	75,000.00
D2	**Router configuration :** 1. Leased Line Modem Configuration. 2. Connectivity through Modem 3. Router configuration for Leased Line connectivity.	NA	

Sr. No.	*Description*	*Qty.*	*Cost*
D3	**Network Security** : 1. Firewall Design & Implementation. 2. IP Filtering based on Customer's requirements. 3. V-LAN configuration for added security.	NA	58,64,750.00

2. Software

Sr. No.	*Description*	*Qty.*	*Cost*
PART - A – OPERATING SYSTEM SOFTWARE			
A1	Windows NT 4 Server OEM Pack (5 User Licenses)	1	29,000.00
PART - B – APPLICATION SOFTWARE			
B1	MS Office 2000 Suit Premium	1	25,000.00
B2	Visual Basic 6.x with MSDN	1	25,000.00
PART - C – ANTI -VIRUS SOFTWARE			
C1	Norton Anti-Virus 2001	1	10,000.00
			89,000.00

Total Hardware Cost	Rs. 58,64,750.00
Total Software Cost	Rs. 89,000.00
Approx. Project Cost	Rs. 59,53,750.00

Note :-

1. Above mentioned quantities of Active and Passive Networking Components may vary at the time of actual implementation of project.
2. Cable prices calculated considering approximate distances, which may vary at the time of implementation according to actual measured distances.
3. Above prices are taken from MNC brand company and the prices quoted here are as per the price list of August-2001.

Organization Chart of the University

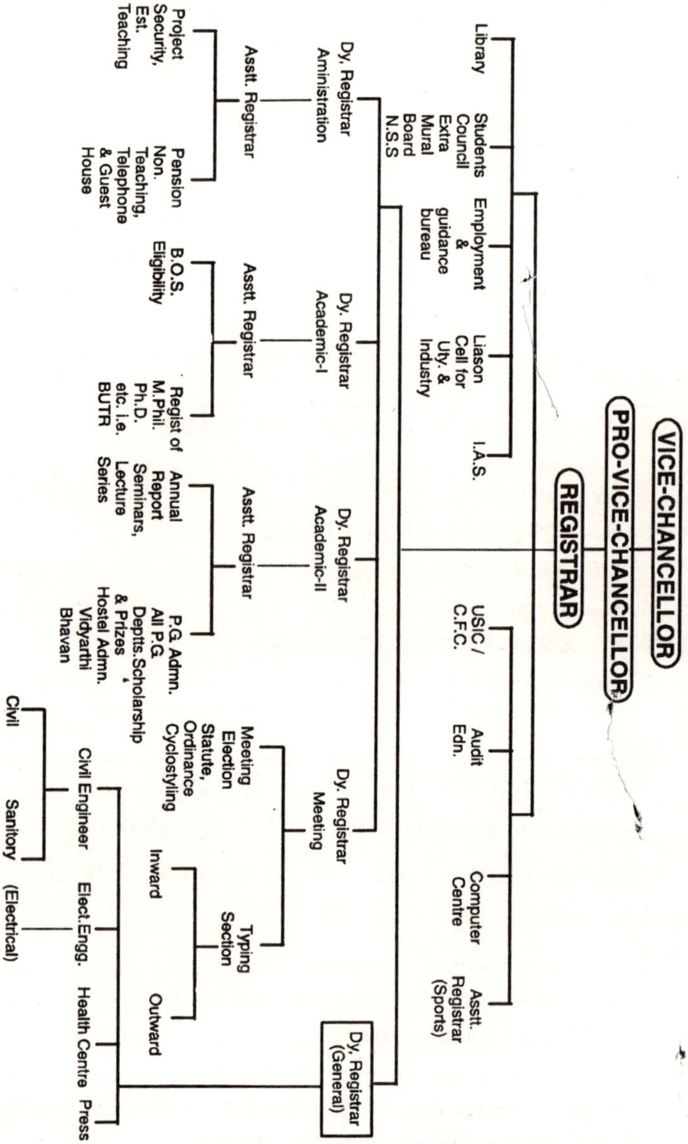

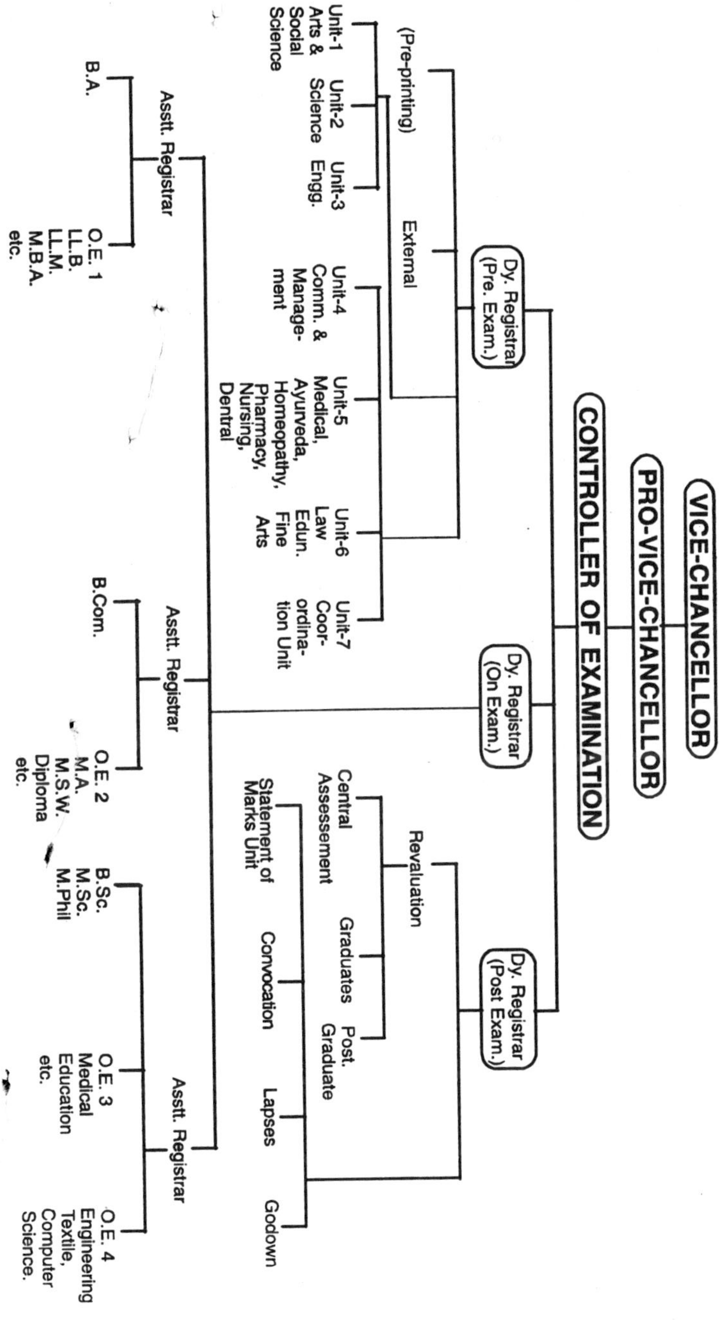
VICE-CHANCELLOR
PRO-VICE-CHANCELLOR
CONTROLLER OF EXAMINATION
Dy. Registrar (Pre. Exam.)
Dy. Registrar (On Exam.)
Dy. Registrar (Post Exam.)
(Pre-printing)
External
Unit-1 Arts & Social Science
Unit-2 Science
Unit-3 Engg.
Unit-4 Comm. & Manage-ment
Unit-5 Medical, Ayurveda, Homeopathy, Pharmacy, Nursing, Dental
Unit-6 Law Edun. Fine Arts
Unit-7 Coor-ordina-tion Unit
Asstt. Registrar
B.A.
O.E. 1 LL.B. LL.M. M.B.A. etc.
Asstt. Registrar
B.Com.
O.E. 2 M.A. M.S.W. Diploma etc.
Asstt. Registrar
B.Sc. M.Sc. M.Phil
O.E. 3 Medical Education etc.
O.E. 4 Engineering Textile, Computer Science.
Revaluation
Central Assessement
Graduates
Post. Graduate
Statement of Marks Unit
Convocation
Lapses
Godown

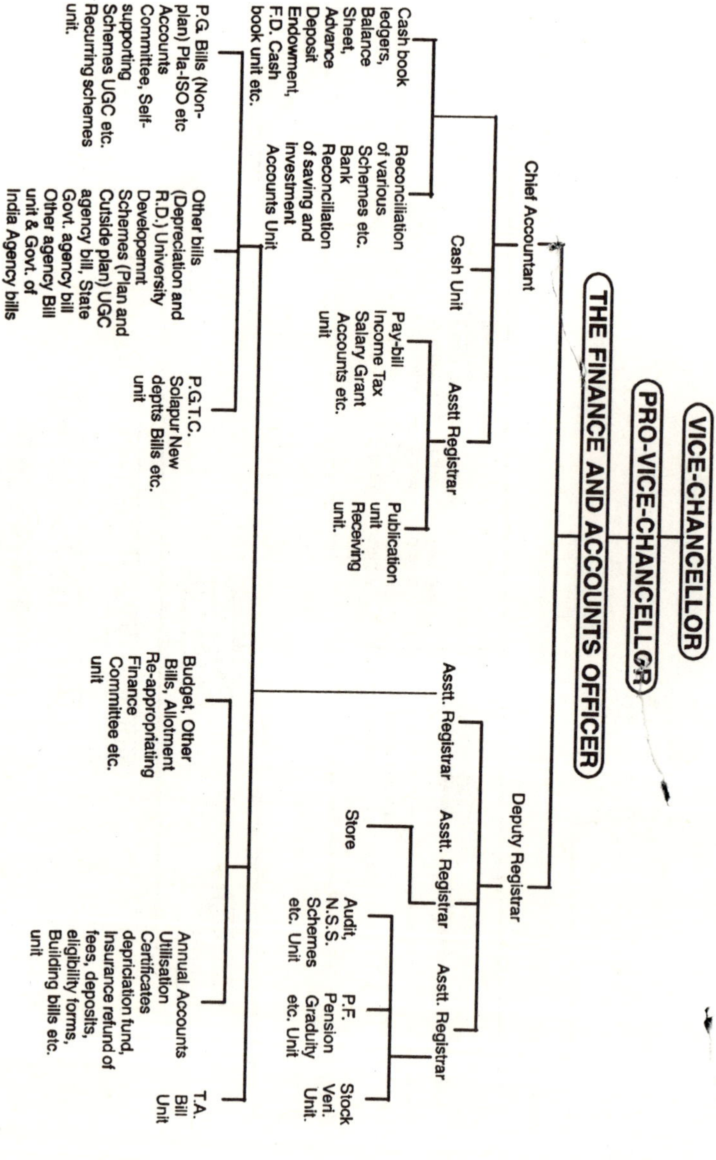
VICE-CHANCELLOR
PRO-VICE-CHANCELLOR
THE FINANCE AND ACCOUNTS OFFICER
Chief Accountant
Cash Unit
Asstt Registrar
Cash book ledgers, Balance Sheet, Advance Deposit Endowment, F.D. Cash book unit etc.
Reconciliation of various Schemes etc. Bank Reconciliation of saving and investment Accounts Unit
Pay-bill Income Tax Salary Grant Accounts etc. unit
Publication unit Receiving unit.
P.G. Bills (Non-plan) Pla-ISO etc Accounts Committee, Self-supporting Schemes UGC etc. Recurring schemes unit.
Other bills (Depreciation and R.D.) University Developemnt Schemes (Plan and Cutside plan) UGC agency bill, State Govt. agency bill Other agency Bill unit & Govt. of India Agency bills
P.G.T.C. Solapur New deptts Bills etc. unit
Deputy Registrar
Asstt. Registrar
Asstt. Registrar
Asstt. Registrar
Store
Audit, N.S.S. Schemes etc. Unit
P.F. Pension Gradulty etc. Unit
Stock Veri. Unit.
Budget, Other Bills, Allotment Re-appropriating Finance Committee etc. unit
Annual Accounts Utilisation Certificates depriciation fund, Insurance refund of fees, deposits, eligibility forms, Building bills etc. unit
T.A. Bill Unit

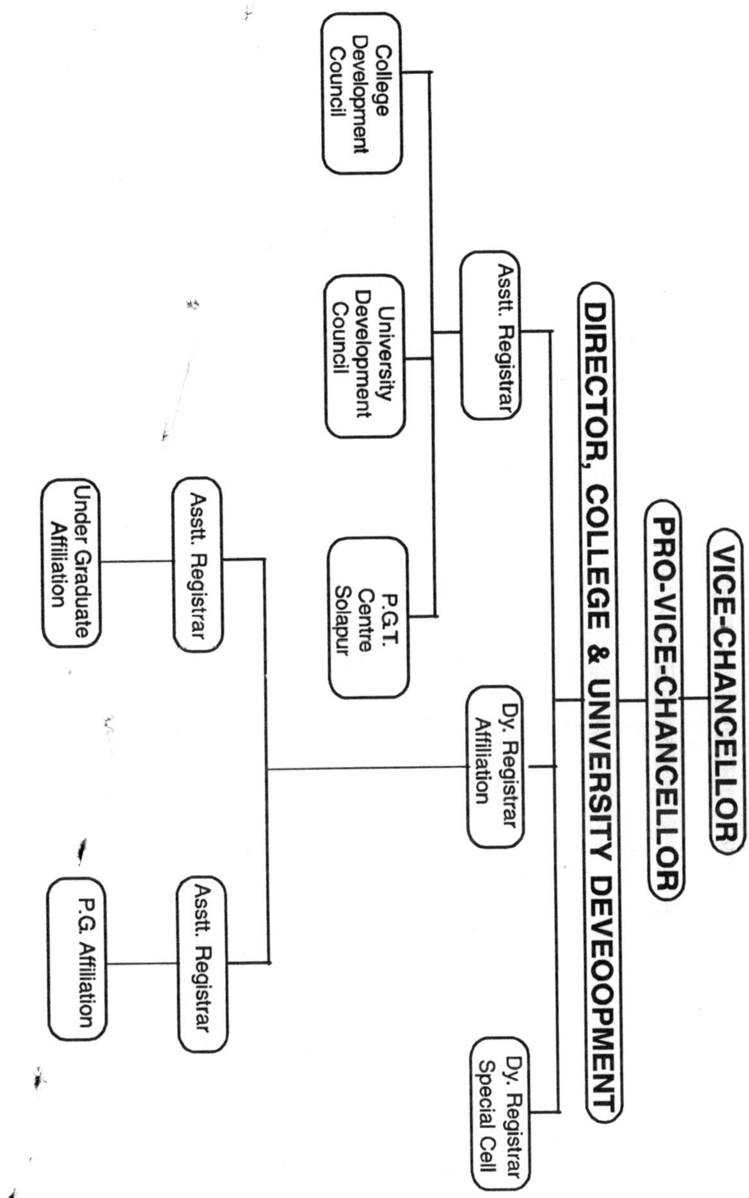
VICE-CHANCELLOR
PRO-VICE-CHANCELLOR
DIRECTOR, COLLEGE & UNIVERSITY DEVEOOPMENT
Asstt. Registrar
Dy. Registrar Affiliation
Dy. Registrar Special Cell
College Development Council
University Development Council
P.G.T. Centre Solapur
Asstt. Registrar
Asstt. Registrar
Under Graduate Affiliation
P.G. Affiliation

9
Conclusions and Suggestions

ABSTRACT

In this chapter the researcher has made the final conclusions of research, observations, advantages and suggestions. Researcher has come to this conclusions after a detail study of use of MIS in University Administration.

9.1. CONCLUSIONS

9.1.1. Introduction

The researcher has analysed at length the working of university and day-to-day need of information for university administration. The present chapter makes an attempt to review the important findings and then offer meaningful suggestions for necessary modifications in the existing system so as to place them on a sound footing and as guidelines.

9.1.2. General observations

From the earlier study on university administration and through the discussions with Hon. Vice-Chancellor, Controller of Examination, Finance &Accounts Officer,

Registrar and Director Board of College and University Development and Deputy Registrars the researcher realized that all the four major sections of university share same information for various purposes.

The top management people in the university needs up-to-date information for decision making. In many cases the decision has to be taken in very short period and for this they need a speedy, accurate and reliable information system to assist them in decision making.

From the study of the use of Management Information System for University Administration, it is observed that the management of the university at various levels gets reliable and quick information about all sections and aspects which it can use for any decision making purpose. Computerised system ensures accuracy and further helps in speedy analysis of data, drawing of graphs, preparation of estimates/projections, storage of data for future use, transfer of data from one section to another section, one university to another university through electronic media which helps in reduction of stationary cost and time. Similarly a password protection can be used to ensure confidentiality of important data.

In general it is observed during the course of study that the maintenance of Information System in decision making process has not received adequate attention in all universities. Management did not give much attention to use of information system because of the lack of cost awareness. As a result delay in decision making could not be avoided. In most of the universities it is observed that the officers of different levels are following a practice of taking decisions based on intuition and situation management, rather than following a scientific approach. In general management is not having cost consciousness.

9.1.3. Advantages

Thus, it is observed that the universities will work more efficiently if they use Management Information System.

Following are the main advantages of Management Information System for University administration : –

1. The university staff is relived from doing cumbersome calculations.
2. The software is designed such that it can be run on LAN or stand alone machine.
3. The software also provide graphical reports to understand the growth of particular faculty in graphical manner.
4. The software is developed in Latest GUI (Graphical User Interface) technology by using Visual Basic-6 which is menu driven and any lay-man with little knowledge of computer can use the software.
5. The software is menu driven and thus, the computer user need not remember the name of program to run and thus it avoids unnecessary memorizing of the program name by the computer user and any chance of making mistakes.
6. A user can do the processing any number of times. It will not tamper the files.
7. Security checks are imposed for unauthorized access
8. Restricted access to confidential data

9.1.4. Findings

We have confined this study for the design and development of computerized information System. The study examines the flow of information within the university. The researcher has visited all the sections of the university and observed their working in detail and interviewed the staff for their requirements in the new

Management Information System

University organization is divided into four parts

* General Administration
* Examination
* Affiliation
* Finance & Accounts

1. It is observed during the course of study that designing of internal organisation structure did not receive adequate attention in some of the universities. The span of control basis of departmentation, demarcation between line and staff, their job description and functions are not clearly specified.

   As a result the information needs, reporting, responsibilities and information flow could not be accurately identified in the organisation structure.

2. In most of the universities it is found that the organisation arrangement for MIS are too inadequate and enough attention has not been given to this aspect. There are no clear-cut procedures for collection, recording processing, presentation and retrieval of data pertaining to crucial organisational functions.

   As a result there is no regular flow of information for decision making at different levels of organisation. However, in actual practice, the information for decision is made available only on pressures and repeated demands.

3. In most of the universities it is found that staff at different levels are following a practice of taking decisions based on intuition and situation management rather than following a scientific approach as a result there is a general phenomenon

of lack of data consciousness among managers / executives in universities.

4. In almost all the universities, EDP has been introduced and computers are already installed. Through the computers are put to some use, the MIS has not been designed appropriately as per the requirements of information technology.
5. It has been observed that there is a great deal of misconception about an information system in almost all universities particularly at middle and lower level management.
6. These must be a sound database and separate data banks for each and every department to enter the needs of data and to maintain the proper flow of data.

9.2. Suggestions

Having given the important findings, now outline the suggestions and recommendations which might help the University administration in better management of their resources.

Following suggestions are made :-

1. With the use of scanners, photos of important events held in the university history can be stored on computer and same can be produced on screen or on paper when required.
2. To speed up the data collection, data entry, processing and reporting work by utilising the computers to the optimum level
3. A separate MIS department should be setup in University and all the information should be routed through MIS Department.
4. To reduce repetitive work of statements / reports preparation which are required for different

purposes such as reports to state Govt., UGC, New Delhi etc. The common reports and data can be routed through the Information System.

5. To prepare an operational manual, define clearly the procedures, duties and responsibilities at each level of management. This will help the new staff to get the idea about the organisational policies immediately on joining the duties. This will also insure the staff accountability in the organisation.

6. Proper training to all levels of management regarding computer awareness should be given by the university.

7. University should maintain a centralised 'Data Bank' to store data and retrieve the same when required.

8. The researcher has suggested a University campus wide network in Chapter No. 7 with approximate costing of Hardware and Software.

9. Explain the advantages and need of computerisation to all staff members.

10. Try to use existing hardware.

11. Ask for more funds from UGC and State Govt. for MIS development in universities.

12. An attempt was made by Pune University to develop MIS is failed due to following reasons :-

    i. Lack of training to non-teaching staff.

    ii. Software development work was assigned to outside party.

    iii. Outside party developing MIS software deputed less man power to study and development of MIS.

    iv. Lack of planning and co-ordination among the sections.

v. Less funds with Universities.

vi. Resistance form unions for computersation.

9.3. Conclusion

University can implement MIS by installing MIS server in the central location and connecting all nodes at different sections and departments by using fiber and UTP cabling, switch and hubs.

The Management Information System developed for university administration is helpful to the top management people while taking decisions and also to the other staff members.

Initial feed backs collected by researcher from various users for the study have been positive. The university officers have certainly stated that this system can be employed to expedite decision process and thereby save time, though the system can be employed in the present state, another round of quick study of exact requirements of the universities and then the system can be customized and put to use for real life situations.

Bibliography

1. Information Management Systems, concepts structure and Development by Dr. P.C. Jain
2. Organisation and Management by R.D. Agarual
3. MIS Concepts and Design by Murdick Munson
4. University Management and Administration by Yoginder S. Verma
5. Systems Analysis and Design by Perry Eduards
6. Database Management Systems by Raghu Ramkrishnan
7. Maharashtra State Universities Act-1994 publish by Govt. of Maharashtra
8. Management by Information System by Joel E. Ross.
9. Information System : Concepts for Management by Lucas
10. Data Processing and MIS by Anderson, Mc Donald, Evans
11. MIS Tools and Techniques by Bocchino William A
12. Information Technology in Higher Education by 'University News' Journal published by Association of Indian Universities
13. University Grants Commission, New Delhi, Annual Reports

14. Management Information System, Conceptual Foundations, Design, Development and Implementations by W. S. Jawadekar
15. Visual Basic 6.0 Complete Reference by BPB Publications
16. Computer Technology for higher education Vol – I, II, III by W. David Chandler, Barbara Kaltz, Murray Kunttila, R. Brien Maguire, William A. stahl, Larry R. Symes published in 1993.
17. Information System Development, Methodologies, Techniques and Tools by D.E. Avison and g. Fitzgerald published in 1988.

Index